FINDING OUT ABOUT THE INCAS

finding out about
THE INCAS

by Cottie A. Burland

illustrated with photographs
and with drawings
by Edward Shenton

Lothrop, Lee and Shepard Co. Inc.,   New York

table of contents

the people of peru

Who were the Incas and what were they really like?

From accounts left by the Spaniards who conquered them in 1533, we know that they were a race of South American Indians whose remarkable civilization in the highlands of Peru endured for over five hundred years!

One of the oldest written sources of information about these fascinating people is a very famous manuscript of nearly twelve hundred pages, written with a quill pen by Guaman Poma de Ayala in the late Sixteenth and early Seventeenth centuries.

Poma de Ayala was the son of a great Peruvian nobleman, a descendant of Inca princes. After the Spanish conquest of Peru, Poma's father became a Christian. He was made a grandee by the Spanish and given the title "Don Felipe."

When Poma de Ayala was growing up, Don Felipe took him to all the places famous in Inca history. They went up into the mountains to the place where the ancestors of the Incas had first arrived in Peru on the orders of their father, the sun god. Poma saw the palaces and fortresses of the capital city, Cuzco, and visited the wonderful Coricancha temple where the sun god used to live. Sometimes Don Felipe was allowed to take his son into the houses where ancient boards with the history of the Incas painted on them were kept. Young Poma de Ayala also saw many paintings that showed the Spanish conquest.

He must have loved these stories and pictures and kept them in his mind, for when he was a grown man and a clever lawyer living in Spain, he wrote his book and drew the pictures of things he remembered or had heard about. He told as best he could the story of faraway Peru.

In 1616, when he was growing old, he presented the book to King Philip III of Spain. It had taken him from 1587 to 1613 to write it. Some later Spanish ruler presented the book as a gift to the King of Denmark and today it is in the collection of the Royal Library in Copenhagen. But not until 1908 did scholars and archaeologists realize what an invaluable source book it was for insights into the life and accomplishments of the Incas.

The pictures in Poma de Ayala's book show the people of Inca Peru dressed in their ancient costumes—husbands with their wives, the officers of state, the soldiers and peasants. In the backgrounds are carefully detailed drawings of the objects and household articles of everyday Inca life, from the digging-stick—the Inca plow—to the mysterious Ilautu, the crown of the Inca ruler.

The Indians seen in the drawings were slight in build, but with wiry muscles. They lived and worked on the high plateaus of the Andes. Cuzco, their capital city, was more than nine thousand feet above sea level, and only strong and healthy people could live and work at such an altitude.

Poma shows them as having strangely shaped heads,

Inca farmer using a digging-stick.

but this was not the fault of his drawing. He drew them as they really looked. Babies were put in their cradles with a little board resting lightly on their foreheads. It made their skulls grow high at the back and flat in front. The people said they did this so that it would be easier for the children to wear a carrying-strap around their foreheads when they grew up. And true enough, Poma de Ayala drew grownups carrying heavy loads on their backs, held not by shoulder straps but by a broad band passing across the fore-head of the carrier. But this was also for fashion as well as usefulness, for even the Inca ruling chief had his skull shaped in this way when he was a child. It must have done no harm to the brain inside, for some of the Incas were very brilliant men.

Naturally one expects the Incas themselves to appear somewhat different from the tribes over which they ruled. But for all their stories of a separate origin, Poma de Ayala drew them to look like the other Indians of Peru. As a matter of fact, they had no conception of other types of human beings. There were stories of white-bearded men who lived in the mythical past when the sacred city of Tiahuanaco was built, but until the Spaniards arrived, no Peruvian Indian had actually seen a white man.

The drawings show the members of the Inca family dressed like the other Indians, but with more decoration on their clothing. We have to turn to the Spanish chroniclers to understand this. They tell us that the Incas were dressed in "chumpi," a cloth made from the delicate wool of the wild vicuna. This was incomparably more delicate and beautiful than the cloth made from the wool of the alpaca which ordinary people wore. Common llama wool was too coarse to be used for weaving in Peru, for these highlanders demanded a finer fabric.

The Inca costume was very simple. Men wore leg garments resembling pantaloons drawn in above the knee, and a tunic made out of two oblong pieces of cloth joined at sides and shoulders, rather like a sack, with holes for arms and head. This was gathered in

Tunic woven in a typical Inca geometric design.

13

at the waist by a broad belt that went around the wearer two or three times.

The belt was very important to the Inca, because the colored patterns woven in it showed his position in society. The Inca wore a belt with different patterns for every different ceremony he performed. It was the same for other men, down to the simplest farmers in the little plots of land on the mountainside. They wore plain belts on ordinary days and brightly colored embroidered ones on festival days.

The farmers and other workers in Inca Peru wore sandals made of llama hide. The sandals had thick, strong soles made from many layers of leather, and were held in place by a thong between the big toe and the other toes, which looped into a strap going across the instep; an ankle strap was fixed to the back of the sandal. Young warriors of the Inca family wore shoes made of a special grass which looked almost like gold after it was dried. The chronicles tell us that the Inca ruler himself wore sandals made of real gold, but Poma's drawings do not tell us anything about the material—only that they were toe-strap sandals like all other sandals in Peru.

Women wore sandals of the same kind. Their long dresses were made like a broad sack, reaching from the shoulders to the ankles. This gown was usually made of plain material, decorated with bands of tapestry at neck and hem. They also wore tight belts, bound several times around the waist. Their head covering was a piece of cloth, folded two or three times on top and hanging down behind to a point just below the shoulders. When going out they often wore long, wide cloaks which were held together at the neck by large, decorated silver pins.

The word "Inca" was used not only for the specific tribe or family, but for its ruler as well. The ruling Inca and his queen, the Coya, were dressed much the same as other people, but in more gorgeous materials. Fine wools in the most vivid colors made their costumes appear as splendid as Chinese silks.

All their ornaments were of gold, for gold was the sacred metal of the sun. Only members of the Inca family might wear it, because they alone were the descendants of the sun god, Inti.

The headcloth of the queen was made of the purest white wool. The headdress of the Inca was made of scarlet wool ribbons wound several times around his forehead; on the front of it he wore the sacred llautu. On a short stick about six inches high there was a flat tassel of scarlet wool like a little banner, and above that two small feathers of brilliant yellow. These feathers came from a rare bird that lived only in one remote valley of the Andes.

The Indians of Peru believed that the Creator made only one pair of these birds for each Inca, so that the two feathers on the llautu were really a gift to the Child of the Sun from the great Viracocha himself. This was the way with many things in ancient

15

Peru—the simplest object could be used as a symbol for an important idea. In this case the two yellow feathers were more important than all the gold in the Inca empire.

It is almost impossible for us to realize the splendor of the Incas in their own days. On a great festival day in Cuzco the narrow streets flanked by gray stone walls must have glittered with splendid costumes and headdresses from all parts of the kingdom. Chiefs and their servants from places as far apart as Quito in Ecuador and the river Maule in Chile would flock to the side of their lord, the Supreme Inca, whenever he held his great festivals. Indians from the cities of the Peruvian coast and befeathered savages from the Amazon jungle joined in these throngs from the Four Quarters of the Earth (Tahuantinsuyu), as they called the Inca Empire.

Among them were the nobles, the members of the Inca family. These were distinguished from all other people by their great golden ear-discs which glittered like suns, often so big as to touch the shoulders. There were many thousands of these members of the Inca clan. All were descended from one or other of the previous ruling Incas through two or three hundred junior wives which each Inca brought into his family, as well as from the queen. These Incas could never become Topa Inca, or Emperor, but they all held high positions in the state.

All these people appear in the pages of Guaman

A group of Incas on their way to a festival in Cuzco.

Poma's manuscript, though he was not able to present them in color. But apart from his chronicles, and others written by Spaniards and Indians who had known the Peru of the Incas, we have the records of archaeology.

By the time that Poma de Ayala's book came to light in the Royal Library in Copenhagen, archaeologists were beginning to realize that ancient Peruvian pottery showed many different styles which could not all have been made in one historical period. They were becoming convinced that Peruvian history might well go back for a thousand years before the first Inca. (Today we know that there were skilled potters at work in Peru near Chavín two thousand years before the Incas came.) But with Poma de Ayala's sketches to guide them, it became much easier to identify some of the types of pottery that were used in Inca times.

By comparing their pots with others, it appeared that the Peruvians of the Inca homeland in the mountains had a special way of painting their pots and utensils. They preferred a geometric arrangement of lines, and occasionally decorated a vase with painted flowers. Also the quality of their pottery was much the finest in Peru. They made simple shapes, such as the ones in Poma's drawings, by molding them from coils of clay, without a potter's wheel. They rarely used molds for shaping their pots, although other peoples on the coast of the Pacific were molding almost all their pots at that period.

The comparison of pot designs, and the sketches

(a, b, c) Three Inca pottery vessels decorated with similar painted designs. (d) A small ladle decorated with a design of painted llamas.

of costumes in Poma's drawings, enabled us to identify typical Inca patterns on ancient textiles also, and so to give them a date.

In the rocky soil of the Peruvian highlands, archaeologists have found very little except the typical Inca pottery and the great stone walls of ruined buildings. In Cuzco itself, many of the foundation walls of Inca palaces are still standing. Part of the Coricancha, the golden temple of the Sun, remains as the foundation of the church of Saint Dominic. However, the dating of stone walls is, in most cases, dependent on the finding of pottery in connection with them. We are quite sure of the styles of Inca pottery. The pots of the last period of the civilizations of the Peruvian coast are like the pottery drawn in the book of Guaman Poma, and these in turn are like the more colorful pottery of the highland sites of the Inca period. But the stone walls of Peru have been built in many different styles.

The two most important methods of building in ancient Peru were based on an intimate knowledge of stone cutting. There are walls whose lower sections are made up of enormous blocks of stone which have been given smooth faces. Their sides have been cut to sharp angles, as close as possible to the original contours of the block. Into these angles other stones have been exactly fitted, with the angles cut very carefully and smoothed down, so that they present the appearance of a crazy-paving path stood up on end. But instead of being small blocks, these stones

Stonework in a section of the wall of Coricancha, the sun temple in Cuzco.

may weigh many tons, and it must have taken dozens of men to move them into position.

The other style of building used carefully squared blocks weighing about fifty pounds each. These were cut and prepared in quarries, then brought to the building site and used as if they were ordinary bricks. Archaeologists used to think that these two styles of building belonged to two different periods, but as soon as they were able to identify the buildings from the chronicles, it became clear that both styles were used by the stonemasons of late Inca times. Inca period potsherds have been found under both types of wall.

Through the gray stone streets of the Inca cities Guaman Poma often walked with his father. For him there was no puzzle about the age of the walls. He noted the wonderful size of the huge stones which were used in them. But his greatest interest was in his father's stories of the Incas, their customs and ceremonies. For him their world was one not long departed, and its glories still echoed in the shadows of the great walls. He knew well that the Inca Empire was the last of a long series of civilizations, and he drew pictures of its traditions in his book.

But the story which archaeology has revealed during the past fifty years is far more fascinating than the traditional accounts of early Peru.

before the incas

GUAMAN POMA has drawn pictures about "the four ages of Peru." His First Age was a time when men used sticks and stones to hunt wild beasts for food. They dressed in skins and lived in shelters made of tree boughs, or in lean-to huts fashioned from reeds.

How right he was! But he never imagined that there had been people living this way in Peru at least twenty thousand years before him. That we know so much today is due to the many scientists from all over the world who became interested in early Peru.

This interest was not an ancient one, but quite a modern attitude of mind. For three centuries after the Spanish conquest, nobody was very much concerned about the past. So long as Peru was a Spanish colony, the men who ruled it were only interested in the silver mines of Potosí, and in shipping their treasures back to Spain. Later, when Peru became a republic, there was a great struggle to improve social conditions in the country and create new institutions.

These were the days of increasing trade in metals, and the beginning of close commercial relations between Peru and the United States, as well as with Great Britain and Germany. Railways were built, new roads constructed, and Peru became a flourishing modern nation. But in those busy years the glories of the Inca past were almost forgotten, and very few people indeed were able to get down to serious archaeological work.

Baron von Humboldt (1769-1859) had traveled through the Peruvian highlands, reporting on the wonders of geography and natural history and the remains of Inca buildings. An English sea captain had brought back some strange wood carvings found deep under fifty feet of sea bird droppings (guano) on an islet off the Peruvian coast. The German travelers, Reiss and Stübel, had produced an illustrated report of their very careful excavations of a great pre-Inca cemetery at Ancon, and thus people came to know of the archaeological treasures still to be found in Peru. But this knowledge was disconnected.

Meanwhile the cemeteries continued to be pillaged by grave robbers in search of gold. These *huaqueros*, as they were called, were equipped with long thin rods with which they probed the sands in hopes of locating a burial place. If they found anything that obstructed their probes, they dug it out. Sun-dried mummies were hurled from their graves and their beautifully woven shrouds destroyed in the search for gold ornaments. Pots, too, were taken because they could be sold for a few pesos to visitors who liked to take these "Inca curios" away with them to their homes. Peru was in danger of losing its wonderful past, even before any scientific workers could study it properly.

The interest of Peruvians in their own past was revived by the news of discoveries that archaeologists were making in other countries. The greatest inspiration probably came from the work of Professor W. M. Flinders Petrie in Egypt. The leading Peruvian scholar in the field was Dr. Julio C. Tello. The story goes that Tello was partly of Indian descent, and as a boy sold papers in the streets of Lima. The stories of the past of the Indian people fired his imagination, and he set out to educate himself so that he could study it. His efforts were successful, and in time he was appointed to a junior position in the National Museum of Peru. Finally he became director of the great museum and inspired it with his own eagerness to carry on a scientific study of the past. He made many discoveries but did not always find the answers to the problems that they raised. His work was a foundation upon which many other researchers have been able to build up our present rich knowledge of pre-Inca Peru.

Most of Tello's researches concerned the civilization of the Peruvian highlands. He showed that the influences which spread from Tiahuanaco, near Lake Titicaca in Bolivia, were by no means local affairs, and that they represented something like a highland empire long before the Inca. He placed even earlier the strange culture which, in his day, was known only by a ruined stone temple at Chavín de Huántar. Between these civilizations and the Incas there were many other cultures of a sort, mostly quite small in area, and probably representing tribal confederations rather than empires. It became clear that the Inca was the last of three civilizations which had arisen in the highlands of Peru, and that all three had reached very high levels of skill in working stone.

Tello was also interested in the coastal culture of Peru, and he was able to show the relationship between the Tiahuanaco Empire and the Nasca people of the southern half of the Peruvian coast. In the same way the appearance of Inca art and design among the works of the Chimu peoples of the northern coast proved the truth of the Inca tradition of their conquest of a great coastal empire less than a century before the arrival of the Spaniards.

Work on the coastal settlements of Peru attracted many archaeologists. The desert coast was a good place for finding remains well preserved, because of its constant dryness.

The result of the work of all these men, and many

other scientists and students, has been a new knowledge of the history and growth of ancient Peruvian civilization. It has needed many people to bring the story together, because in Peru there are very few places where one can trace a series of civilizations like that of Troy, or Jericho, or other city sites in the Old World. In Peru each civilization seems to have preferred to start in a new place. So we have depended upon evidences of trade, such as the dried body of a llama foal from the highlands found in a coastal Nasca grave, or the appearance of a southern pot of the Nasca type in a north coast cemetery.

Fortunately for us, all the peoples on the Peruvian coast were harassed by desert conditions. They would not build cities or bury their dead on the well-watered lands where food could be grown, and so their cemeteries are crowded out into areas of sand. Because of this, there are a few cemeteries where one finds graves of several periods with different kinds of pottery in them, and sometimes different kinds of linings to the tombs, usually in the form of mud bricks.

Through such discoveries it has been possible to determine which were earliest and which were latest among the series of civilizations on the Peruvian coast. But it has been reserved till the last few years of atomic research to give us a nearly accurate time scale for these cultures. There is no King List, like that of ancient Egypt, to help us. In fact there was no tradition of the many civilizations which succeeded each other before the Incas unified Peru under one rule.

Our time scale depends upon the radioactive isotope of carbon which has an atomic weight of 14—carbon 14, we call it. The air consists mostly of molecules of oxygen and nitrogen. At very great heights these molecules are bombarded by particles from the sun, and one result is the production of a substance which acts exactly as if it were ordinary carbon, with the exception that it has an atomic weight of 14 instead of 12 and is slightly radioactive. This carbon 14 is soon mixed with other gases in the air, and is eventually absorbed as part of the carbon dioxide breathed in by plants. So all living plants, and also the animals which eat them, contain a little carbon 14 within themselves. When these plants and animals die they absorb no more carbon 14. Carbon 14 is radioactive, and it slowly loses its activity with the passage of time.

Fortunately this loss of energy is very slow, and quite constant in rate. The scientist has to find out how much of the radioactivity has been lost since his archaeological specimens were buried. To do this he takes a sample of skin or hair or bone, or else of wood associated with the specimen he is examining. This is roasted until reduced to charcoal, which is nearly pure carbon. The charcoal is then reduced again to an incandescent carbon dioxide gas which can be examined through the spectroscope to find if carbon 14 is actually present. Then the radioactivity of the specimen is measured. From the amount of radioactivity remaining since the death of the specimen, its age can be estimated.

The estimates are never exact, but are given as an average which is accurate within some fifty years or so, either way. We cannot say, "This wood came from a tree cut down on July 5th, 900 A.D." But the scientist makes his estimate, "This tree died 1,050 years, plus or minus 50 years, B.P. (Before the Present)." He then adds the date of his examination of the specimen and leaves us to work out the range of dates which he had allowed us. In the following pages you will find some dates which come from carbon 14 dating methods. You must be prepared to accept them as close approximations only, and not as exact dates. In the earlier periods they may be a century wrong; in the later, about twenty years.

The result of all this recent scientific work, where the archaeologist and the physicist have joined hands, is a good outline of ancient Peruvian history. It is no more than an outline, but we know that the future will bring more and more discoveries to fill in details. As it stands, the story begins about twenty thousand years ago.

When men were hunting mammoth in Europe, other men were hunting mastodon in Ecuador, a little north of Peru. To the south, in Chile, hunters and fishermen left the remains of their food and several layers of nicely chipped stone tools. They had already been in that part of the world for a long time.

29

The climate of South America seems to have altered somewhat during the ages. The desert belts were probably smaller, and the tropical rain forests of the northern part of the continent seem to have been more easily penetrated by wandering tribes. But we find very little archaeological material in Peru dating back to more than eight thousand years ago. Already at that period we have evidence that far to the north in Mexico the people had begun to cultivate maize, but in Peru there was no trace of agriculture so early.

The story of a little settlement on the Peruvian coast at this time seems to have been very like the story of Jericho at the same period, before agriculture had begun. The Peruvian Indians lived by fishing in the warm waters of the Pacific. They built themselves a settled village, with rectangular houses made of mud bricks. In their graves, under the houses, were found very well-made fishhooks and nets, together with matting but there is no trace of any grains, or any pottery for storing and cooking. Only one such village is known to us. There are probably others, perhaps even the remains of towns to be discovered. But even as it is we know that in South America man was settling down in the well-built villages before he had developed agriculture, and also before he had discovered how to make pottery.

Before we knew anything about the state of civilization on the high plateau of the Andes, we knew there must have been people there, cultivating quinoa, and

later, maize, and that there were llamas. This knowledge came from chance finds in the graves of fisherpeople on the Peruvian coasts. These fisherpeople had
developed weaving, and raised beans and pumpkins,
gourds and canes of many kinds. They discovered the
possibilities of the balsa tree for rafts to take them on
fishing expeditions; for in-shore fishing they made
themselves cozy little bathtub-size canoes from bundles of totora reeds. After each fishing trip the little
reed canoes had to be hung up to dry before being
used again. But as their owners could easily carry them
under one arm, there was good reason for making
them.

What was going on in the highlands, we do not

Inca fishermen in a canoe made of totora reeds.

know. Guaman Poma pictures a Second Period in which people discovered the digging-stick and the maize plant under the inspiration of the god Viracocha. It is likely that the highland people lived in villages, grew maize and potatoes, herded their llamas, and obtained fresh meat by hunting. Potatoes were very important in Peru, but were unknown in the rest of the world until after the Spanish Conquest.

It is doubtful if there was much contact between the coastal and the highland tribes of Peru. The people of the hot dry coastland, used to a life at sea level, could not stand the thin cold air of the mountains. On the other hand, the mountain people would soon die in the heavy, heated air of the coastal belt. Probably they traded very little, and then only in some selected places where the river valleys opened from the mountains into the seacoast plain.

It is too much to expect of human nature that these tribes should have lived in peace. There must have been many intertribal fights over fishing rights and water supplies in the coastal region, and about grazing grounds and maize fields in the highlands. Then, about 900 B.C., civilization suddenly came to them. Whether they developed it themselves, or some conquerors brought it down from the north, we do not know. It is strange that it happened about the same time as the development of a true civilization in far-off Mexico. Several serious archaeologists feel that there was some connection between the two events, but it may take a generation of research before we can prove anything. The common factor in these two areas is the use of stone for monumental sculpture, and its dedication to the gods of the earth. In Peru this took the form of terrifying sculptures of puma gods and the gaping jaws of gigantic serpents.

We know now that the first civilization of highland Peru was centered at Chavín, but that in the valley running north toward the Amazon forests there were three or four cities with stone temples and the images of puma and serpent gods. The Chavín culture also had close artistic contacts with Cupisnique on the northern coast. Great numbers of tombs have been found there containing gray pottery decorated with the same designs as those used at Chavín in the mountains.

Simple weaving was known, but none of the elaborate embroideries and tapestries of later times. Houses were built of large oblong mud bricks. There is not a trace of writing, or even of the knotted string quipus used for keeping records in a more advanced period. But these people were skillful workers in gold, making jewelry embellished with the characteristic lion and puma designs.

Did the Chavín culture come up from the coast to the mountains? Or did it arise in a mountain valley on the eastern slopes of the Andes and later spread westward? We do not know. There is a fascinating field for later discovery here.

After the sudden appearance of high cultivation in the north, the next developments were in the south of Peru in the coastal belt. At Paracas a cemetery was discovered which contained the dried bodies of ancient Peruvians seated in their graves, wrapped in a fantastic profusion of wonderfully embroidered cloths. They date from the last two centuries B.C. until a little after the beginning of the Christian era. Associated with the Paracas culture are fine gold work, wooden boxes, and rather simple pottery with scratched outlines of figures, often colored.

The cloths were made of fine cotton grown locally, embroidered with cotton and also llama wool threads which must have come from the highlands in trade.

A sculptured Inca fertility deity.

34

Embroidery covers the whole of these immense cloths as if they were richly patterned carpets. It must have taken the women a very long time to prepare the cloth for a single burial. In fact, it appears that here we have a civilization where there were nobles who could afford to employ people to work for them.

The cloths also tell us of serpent gods, warriors who carried the heads of their enemies, deities of the pepper plant, and a kind of magic fertility serpent with a cat's face. Not far away from Paracas we find the same designs painted in color on beautifully made pottery discovered in a number of sites around Nasca. The Nasca culture used gold, and the warriors carried long throwing sticks with a stone axe-blade set in the midst of the shaft. This was in the early years of our era, but the same strange weapon was used in recent times by the head-hunting Jivaro on the edge of the Amazon rain forest. It makes us wonder if the Nasca culture has any relationship with the other side of the Andes. We shall find out some day. In any case, the Nasca people painted their pots with gods and demons. In later times they included a god with a white beard. This same god was painted on pots from the northern coast.

Meanwhile, just before the Christian era, Tiahuanaco was built on a high plateau more than two miles above sea level, beside Lake Titicaca in Bolivia. It is obvious from its ruins that Tiahuanaco was once the metropolis of a great civilization. Carved slabs of stone litter the site, as well as standing figures, and there is the gateway of the sun in which we recognize a strange Inca god with short tunic and thick belt. His eyes weep tears, and we remember the relationship between the sun god and the rains as he moves across the heavens from south to north. According to one Inca legend, the tears of the sun were the original source of gold.

This god at Tiahuanaco is crowned with a fan of condor heads like rays of light. In his hands he holds condor-headed serpents, no doubt the serpents of the lightning. Around the god is a group of small winged figures with condor heads. Each one kneels, but the wings are extended. The gate is often said to have been a calendar: perhaps the winged figures are representations of the stars moving across the heavens beyond the sun.

Suddenly, about the fourth century A.D., we find the artistic style of the Tiahuanaco sculptures appearing on the coast. This marks the end of the Nasca culture, and leaves its effects on several smaller cultures north of the Nasca region. Montesinos records an Inca story of a race who were rulers in Peru for eighty generations before the Incas. This period seems impossibly long—about two thousand five hundred years—but maybe the legend refers to the Tiahuanaco Empire. For a while Tiahuanaco was supreme in the southern half of Peru, but about A.D. 400 the empire seems to have collapsed.

We have no written traditions to give us a historical

picture. All we know is that the city remained a very sacred place, even in ruin, right through Inca times. Its art disappeared, and the southern cultures of the Peruvian coast never recovered. Nasca and Paracas became graveyards, and the coastal peoples continued life in small towns. They kept on making rather undistinguished pottery and textiles until the Incas absorbed them into their empire.

Meanwhile, near the center of the coast of Peru and not far from the present site of Lima, arose a sacred center for the worship of a creator god who was called Pachacamac. An ancient pyramid temple became the place where the spirit of this creator was supposed to enter into the priests and give oracles. From all parts of Peru the people came here on pilgrimage. Later the Incas realized that Pachacamac was the same as Viracocha, and they also made rich offerings at the shrine. Strangely enough, this great temple was never the center of a political state. Many lesser city-states arose in the neighborhood, all of them with some echo of Tiahuanaco art in their background, but none of them seem to have been absorbed by their neighbors until the great days when the Incas unified all Peru.

On the northern half of the Peruvian coast there had been a long succession of cultures known by the remains of mud-brick buildings and the vast amount of pottery which they produced. Their characteristic vases with loop spouts appear as early as Cupisnique times, when the spouts were so large that they seem to have been coiled around the fingers of the potters. Later, as one civilization succeeded another, the arts and crafts became more refined, until we find pots of almost eggshell thinness made in molds.

After the fall of Tiahuanaco, the peoples of the northern half of the Peruvian coast continued their almost uninterrupted development. It seems as if they had been aware of the Tiahuanaco civilization, but never greatly influenced by it. In the period between the fourth and fifth centuries they produced the Mochica culture, which we have named after the Muchik language spoken in those parts. We know a great deal about them from the paintings on their pottery. They used colored beans for counting, built pyramid temples of mud bricks, and held annual races to see who could first reach the top of the pyramid and bring luck to the crops.

It is quite obvious that these Mochica were a rich and cultured people who worked metal so skillfully that they could make excellent bronzes hard enough to use as knives and chisels. They were workers in gold, and developed the rich silver resources of Peru for the first time. Their pots include magnificent individual portrait heads in clay, which reveal them clearly to us as a typical American Indian group, many of them not unlike the present-day Araucanians in appearance.

But among these pots appear a few puzzling ones representing a man with a long white beard. In some cases he holds a bird that is almost like a domestic fowl. Was this personage the god of some star, bearded like a comet? Or was he, perhaps, a representative of some Polynesian voyager-chief, come by canoe across the wide Pacific, bringing a fowl with him? Or could he have come up the Amazon from an Arab trading ship which had crossed the Atlantic from the West African coast?

Though it seems fantastic, any of these solutions might be possible. That is one of the fascinations of archaeology; a few curious pots may stir up ideas involving half the world. As the Mochica culture developed, the use of silver greatly increased. In fact, it is possible that the popularity of black pottery in the next historic period was due to the fact that when filled with water it looked like tarnished silver.

From about A.D. 1000 to the time of the Incas, the northern Peruvian coastal peoples were united under the rule of a chief known as the Chimu. They were rich beyond all immediate needs. Their cities were large and filled with great square courtyards lined with rooms around a central garden. The rivers were diverted through narrow canals to make every possible square yard of soil yield its best crops. The Chimu had a special court of nobles and officers around him, and he was adorned with magnificent jewelry of gold and silver. In this hot coastal land silver was regarded as especially precious because it symbolized the moon god, who brought coolness of night to the parched country.

The Chimu were great traders and travelers, and it seems, from the researches of Dr. Heyerdahl, that they were familiar with the Galapagos Islands, five hundred miles off the coast of Ecuador. Certainly their pottery has been found there. They were the richest of all the civilizations of Peru until the Incas came, and after that they still remained very wealthy, sending their gold to Cuzco and marrying an Inca princess to the Chimu himself. They are reputed to have been a lazy people, but it seems that they were so well off that they saw no sense in fighting a superior Inca army. War would have brought the burning of towns and the breaking down of the irrigation ditches, and they were willing to pay a tribute in order to avoid this. S just after the middle of the fifteenth century A.D., they rather grudgingly accepted the rule of the Incas over their ancient kingdom.

Up in the highlands of Peru the archaeological record is far less complete. There are many remains of stone buildings and sculpture, but few graves with trade goods, and no stratified sites so far recorded. After the collapse of Tiahuanaco, the great city continued to be a holy place of pilgrimage. The Incas built a sun temple there, and our finest Inca cloth comes from a stone box found in this temple by the French traveler, Bandelier.

The Tiahuanaco-style designs continued, in a much weakened form, through what is called the Pucara (Fortress) culture to the verge of Inca times. At some point the great stone sculptures of Aija Huaraz were made. The Colla people, perhaps the descendants of the builders of Tiahuanaco, erected stone towers with little rooms reached by staircases. In these rooms they stowed away the dried bodies of their dead.

But the puzzle is so complex that one grows sharply aware of the many tribes in this region who were later to become subjects of the Incas. One group, the Yauros, who dwelt in the mountains behind Lima, were great medicine men and healers. They specialized in the treatment of skull injuries. They left behind them not only many skulls skillfully trepanned by removing a section of bone, but also skulls which showed a healthy growth of new tissue to replace the damaged parts. That art was very valuable in a country where the principal weapon was a bronze-headed mace.

It was about the middle of the eleventh century that the Incas are supposed to have appeared upon the scene. According to their own legends, they came from the east. With them they carried a wedge of gold, and wherever they stopped, they laid the wedge upon the ground. At last the wedge sank from sight in the spot where a beautiful valley marked their future home, Cuzco, the Navel of the Earth.

At first only two Incas controlled Hanan Cuzco (Upper Cuzco). They were important tribal chiefs ruling part of the city, rather than the divine rulers of a nation.

It was the danger of raids by neighboring tribes

which led the people of Cuzco to choose the Inca to rule the whole city. Later, the need to protect it still further led the fourth Inca to conquer the entire valley in which the city was situated. It was at this point that the Chanca confederacy of tribes decided to destroy the new power, and failed miserably. The next threat came from the Collas, who ruled the mountain plateaus north of Tiahuanaco. This brought about a bitter war but in the end the Incas emerged victorious, and found themselves the undisputed rulers of the highland plateau of Peru.

From that moment their path was clear. Their father, the sun, had made them emperors as well as a sacred family. Their duty was to extend the faith in sun worship and the blessings of Inca-organized government to the Four Quarters of the Earth. Tahuantinsuyu was the name of their realm—the Four Quarters—and at the time of the arrival of the Spaniards it was two thousand miles long and five hundred miles wide in the deepest section just north of Cuzco.

Such an empire was unknown before in the history of Peru. For the first time the country's many peoples were united. In this union their separate histories were lost until the patient piecing together of puzzles buried in the earth restored some outline of their former glories.

the center of gold

LET US IMAGINE we are making a visit to the Inca capital, Cuzco.

First we go up the hill to the Hawk's Nest, Sacsahuaman, which guards the road into the city. In the center of the walls is a low circular tower which was there in olden times. The view is fantastic, with gray ranges of mountains rising in the distance, and a bowl-like valley below, through which a tumbling little river runs between the rocks. On the slope above the river is Cuzco, the wonderful city.

If we could join the circling condors gliding lazily overhead, we should look down on the thatched roofs clustering here and there around a courtyard, on the narrow streets which make their way straight up to

43

the open space in front of the Coricancha, the "House of Gold."

On one side in the valley is the level field where the Inca might review his troops. Here, also, the brave young men competed for prizes of honor in the yearly examinations given to warriors of Inca blood. To our minds Cuzco seems a small and crowded place, where only ten or twenty thousand people could be collected together, but to the people of Inca times, this was the holy city of an empire whose ruler was descended from the sun.

The gray stone walls of the houses were topped by rounded roofs of thatch which was four feet thick and kept the buildings cool by day and warm by night.

It was not a walled city, but every house could easily become a fortress because of the strength of its masonry. The atmosphere must have been very forbidding to the stranger. The narrow streets were only wide enough for two loaded llamas to pass, steep and unrelieved by decoration or color. Each building faced inward to its courtyard, and to the street it presented a wall of stone, impenetrable and secretive. Perhaps the colored doorways offered an occasional glimpse of the brilliance within, but this was not for the stranger. On festival days the city was crowded, but the buildings were open only to those people who had a right to enter them. The mass of visitors camped out, like a multicolored army, in tents and bivouacs along the valley. The army itself camped on the exercise field,

*The ruins of the pleasure palace of Tampu Machay. Note how
the Inca masons fitted a great natural boulder into their masonry.*

and many of the soldiers were stationed in the Hawk's Nest fortress.

Many of the buildings in Cuzco were government offices. Here dwelt the representatives of the various regions of the empire. Princes from each of the conquered peoples were held in Cuzco as hostages, but they were given every freedom. They had a good allowance of food and fine clothing, were taught the official Quechua language, and shown exactly how the Inca system of government worked. The Incas believed that their methods were the best in the world for bringing prosperity and happiness to the people, so they had no fear of teaching their system to hostages. It helped convert them to the Inca way of life.

A little palace for a hostage prince was arranged around the central courtyard, where there were patches of carefully tended flowers and plants. The kind mother symbol, the maize, grew there, and the many charming alpine flowers of Peru, including petunias. At one side of the courtyard was the hall, together with some smaller sleeping rooms for the prince, his wives and attendants. A bed was a simple pile of soft rugs and coverlets. Clothes were not hung up, but put away carefully in big carved wooden chests, which were painted and decorated with mastic inlay. The hall had a raised throne on which the prince would squat with his feet above the ground. There were lower seats for the lesser people of the household.

Tables were very low, because one ate from them

while sitting on cushions on the floor. There were cups and beakers, together with platters and dishes, made of beaten silver or lacquered wood. The floor was covered with fine reeds, and the thatch above reflected the light straw color. Windows were small, if any, and most light came through the wide doorways. On the grim stone walls were hung brilliant tapestries patterned with many colors arranged in a regularly changing order. In niches on the wall were boxes of personal belongings, and also ornaments of silver and bronze with decorations in colored featherwork.

In the wings of the courtyard there were ranges of small single-story buildings, where the women could spend their time weaving, and workmen carved wood and shaped metal. Some of the offices were occupied by the Quipu-camayoc, who was responsible for keeping countless files of knotted cord quipus. These were made up in colors, which denoted the nature of the records, and filed in chests so that they could easily be taken out and read. The records of such an office were all about the production of food and clothing, and the numbers of people in the home provinces. Every now and then a summary was made; this was sent to the Keepers of Records of the Inca, and a duplicate copy kept in the files at home.

That was one of the secrets of Inca success; all records were kept in a truly businesslike way, so that if information was wanted it could quickly be found. The keeping of his records was a good training for a tribal

Ancient quipu, recording numbers running into tens of thousands.

prince, for one day he would become a tribal chief and go home, where he would be responsible for keeping up a steady supply of records for the central government offices in Cuzco.

At the end of the courtyard nearest the entrance there would be a few round stone buildings with the usual thatch domes. The doors were very small, and always carefully barred, for these were the storehouses in which sacks of food were kept—maize, quinoa, and potatoes for the consumption of the household. Each day some fresh meat or fish was brought in from the markets, but grain and potatoes were the staple foodstuffs. There were also other storehouses in which the official allowance of clothing for the men and women of the household was kept.

Around other courtyards stood the homes and offices of various state officials. There was no dashing away from the office at night for these men. They worked for the Inca, and the Inca fed and clothed them and maintained them in these palaces. They were allowed to have no separate life of their own. It appears that they were quite content with this. They would have enjoyed no more personal freedom if they had been simple farmers, and working and living in Cuzco seemed to them a wonderful reward for serving the Inca so well.

All the higher officials were members of the Inca family, and lived in Cuzco as in their home towns. Everywhere they could be seen, flaunting their fine clothes and golden ear-discs. People bowed to them with great respect. These were the distant relatives of the Sun. Yet they were not useless drones in the hive of the Inca Empire. They were leaders in war, judges, organizers in all branches of the national life. People said that these lesser members of the Inca family were above the law, but that was not quite true. They were not taken before the courts or publicly punished, but if one of them was foolish enough to dishonor the good name of Inca, he would be sent to some dangerous frontier outpost. He might even disappear from public life. Later on, his carefully dried body would have its place in the family mausoleum.

A number of palaces in Cuzco were owned by no living persons. These were the palaces of the dead Topa Incas. Each palace had its full set of officials and servants, its supplies of fine gold cloth and delicate food. The people believed that some day the dead Incas would return to life again, and they awaited this return with eagerness and affection. The bodies remained in the Coricancha, but once a year they were brought to the palaces and treated with all the ceremonies to which they had been accustomed in life.

The Inca was the least free of all the Peruvians. His title, "Topa Inca," meant Only Inca. He was expected to behave like a direct descendant of the Sun. His every action was noted, and he enjoyed little peace and quiet in which to do just as he wished. If he wanted to go walking in his garden, his feet were not allowed to touch the earth, for servants spread down wonderful cloths before him. The very plants and flowers of the palace garden were transmuted by some dreadful Midas touch into flowers of gold and silver. If he wished to drink the sweet maize beer for refreshment, it was poured first into a silver vessel for a servant to taste lest it be poisoned, and then put into a beaker of gold for him to drink. In fact, he might even have to recline as gracefully as he could while a servant poured the drink through a golden tube into the sacred lips of his divine majesty.

The Inca could not even choose his wife. The Coya must be his own sister, because the Children of the Sun must be of pure sun descent on both sides of the family. His other wives were usually chosen for him; they were either the daughters of chiefs who must become royal wives for political reasons, or else too-well-educated young ladies, taught in the strict convent of the Daughters of the Sun. Perhaps the Inca kept some of his dreams for himself, but there was always a soothsayer near at hand to interpret the meaning of the royal dreams for the benefit of the nation.

Once a year he was free. He entered the temple of the Sun on the morning of the festival of the Capac Raymi, took off his turban and llautu, kicked off his golden sandals, and for a while was just a man alone before the image of the Sun and the Creator. Coricancha must have been a house of peace for the divine Inca.

The palace of the Inca was a larger version of the usual stone courtyard house. Its roof was thatched with four feet of golden-yellow grass. The outer wall was made of carefully selected stones laid with great care, so that one of the Spanish conquerors, trying to find out what cement was used to hold the walls together, found that the stones had been ground down so ex-

Ruins of the house of an Inca princess in Macchu Pichu.

actly to fit that he could not get the blade of his steel knife between them. There were no arches in the building, nor in any other in all Peru. Windows were few and high up. They were shaped like the doors, with sides that sloped slightly inward toward the top, and the top itself was a single huge stone lintel.

Within the building, niches in the walls were filled with flowers of gold and silver. The furniture and tapestries were like those in lesser houses, but of far greater magnificence, glittering with golden ornaments and many-colored featherwork. A number of courtyards were included within the palace buildings, so that business could be carried on here as well as in the state apartments.

Stone warehouses surrounded the largest of the courtyards, and these housed great quantities of grain, wool, cotton, dried meat, clothing, armor, and personal weapons. These stores were made up of one third of all the goods produced in the country, and were given to the Inca, but not solely for his personal use. Out of them he had to supply his officials and keep a reserve of material which could be freely distributed in any area where crops had failed or attacks by enemies had destroyed the people's necessary supplies.

Similar palaces housed the priesthood, for there were many priests and priestesses serving under the High Priest, who was usually a brother of the Topa Inca. Only this High Priest was permanently appointed. Others served for a time and were then freed from their duties. They wore no special dress, and seem to have considered it a natural thing to be near their gods and work in the temples. Unfortunately we have no knowledge of their services or of the sun temple which could be entered only by the Inca and the High Priest.

One of the important buildings, whose walls still stand in the narrow streets of old Cuzco, was the House of the Virgins of the Sun. This was a nunnery specializing in all the duties of looking after the temples, and weaving cloth for the temples and the Inca. The Inca alone must have kept several weavers working constantly, because he was never allowed to wear the same dress twice. As soon as he changed his clothes, the old ones, only used once, were whisked away to a special store, where they were kept for use as particularly important gifts to visiting chiefs and favorite noblemen.

The same might happen to the girls in the convent, since they also were valued as presents to be given as wives to great chiefs. These young ladies were selected when about eight years old from any family in any part of the empire. If a girl was exceptionally clever and intelligent as well as beautiful, the local chief was expected to make a report to his town governor, who would in turn send a report to the Inca governor of the province, and he in turn would pass on his selection from the best of all such reports to Cuzco. The princess in charge of the Sun Maidens would consult with the Inca, and then messengers were sent out to bring the selected girl to Cuzco for training.

The great gray Convent of the Sun Maidens was at first a place for hard discipline and learning, but gradually the girls became skilled in their delicate weaving and embroidery, learned the songs in honor of the gods, and were taught how to run a household. No man was ever admitted into this convent except the Inca himself. When the girls went to the temple, they wore special clothes and were set apart as people dedicated to the sun and not to be looked at, much less spoken to, by ordinary folk. They were a group distinct, much more so than the priests. Some were given away by the Inca to be married, but many stayed in the convent all their lives, the white sisters dedicated to the service of the sun.

Beyond their convent, approached through the steep narrow streets, was the great square before the House of the Sun. The holy place of the Incas was a cluster of buildings. There were houses for the moon and stars, a palace for the rainbow and thunder, and smaller temples for all the gods of the subject tribes within the Inca Empire. The stone buildings were quite plain, with the usual heavy thatched roof. But at the end stood Coricancha, marked by the rounded apse at the west end, and a two-foot-broad cornice of gold around the top of the walls outside the building.

There are very few accounts of Coricancha. Its massive walls support the Church of Saint Dominic, but few of the Spanish conquerors saw the interior of this mysterious temple before it was stripped of its colossal treasure to pay a ransom. However, we do know that the walls were lined with deep niches, in each of which squatted the dried mummy of a dead Topa Inca wrapped in his finest clothes and seated on a golden throne. The Spaniards who saw these mummies have told of their wonderful preservation.

At the end of the temple, above the rounded apse of the main wall, was a great relief in gold and emeralds covering the whole end of the building. In the center was the image of the Sun represented with rays around his face. On one side were the morning star and a constellation of small stars above a rainbow, together with the symbols of the Pilcomayo River and the Valley of Cuzco. On the left were the moon, the evening star, the clouds of the sky, and a fox beside a tree.

An empty space represented the creator Viracocha. Below were the stars of Pegasus, and figures of the first man and woman standing beside the place where they were created. These symbols showed the East and the West, and the Central Line of Creation. This was on the meridian of the midnight in August, when the stars passed across the heavens announcing the day when the sun would be vertically overhead in Cuzco. This day was the beginning of the rainy season, and also the occasion of the Situa festival.

The Situa was a very important affair. It began by driving sickness away, and ended by uniting all the people of the empire. At the first new moon in August the Inca and High Priest met with all the nobles and priests of Cuzco in front of the Coricancha. Then and there they decided which of the series of ceremonies should be included and which left out for the coming year.

The announcement of the festival was made on the following morning and the first preparations began. All dogs were driven out of town. Everywhere people were running about the houses, routing out the unfortunate animals, although pets might be sent to the homes of friends at a safe distance. All cripples and sick people were given presents and helped to camps outside the city. These included the members of the Inca family who had been punished by the gods by the tearing of an ear-lobe so that they could not wear their golden ear-discs. Then anyone who was known to have been unlucky during the year went outside the boundaries. Only the people of Cuzco remained in two sections, the Higher Cuzco and the Lower Cuzco. Outside the city still other camps were filling up with strangely dressed foreign tribesmen who had brought their gods to join in the festivities.

The feast opened officially on the next day. On two sides of the square in front of the Coricancha were rows of benches for the people of Hanan Cuzco and Hurin Cuzco, all wearing their war dresses of quilted checkered tunics and copper helmets fringed from ear to ear with feathers.

First there was a review by the Inca, and prayers by the High Priest; then the warriors faced up in four squadrons toward the four points of the compass. At a signal they raced outward along the roads in the four directions, lifting their shields and shouting at an invisible enemy, "Away! Away! All evils away! All sickness away!" At the end of the run they reached rivers into which they plunged, so that all bad luck should be washed off them and dispersed in the distant seas. This was supposed to protect the people from the illnesses of the rainy season.

The second day of the festival was devoted to the gods of the Inca. Again the people of Cuzco attended, men and women wearing their finest clothes. On the far side of the square was a golden bench on which were placed the dead Topa Incas together with their Coyas. They seemed alive in their beautiful robes, but their eyes were cast down as though they meditated on the things of another world. Opposite them sat their descendant, the living Topa Inca, on a golden throne before the gods. The images of the Sun, Rainbow, and Thunder were there; and Huanacauri, a relative of the Inca, a giant turned to stone, was with them.

Prayers were said to the Creator, and then to the other gods, asking for blessings and protection. Next a great bowl of coarse maize porridge was brought in, and everyone came to take a handful of this "Pudding of Divine Protection." From the Inca downwards each one smeared a little on his forehead and then ran to his home with a handful which was spread on the doorpost of the house to protect it from all danger. For the rest of the day the hand, white with porridge, was left unwashed. It was a hand of blessing.

The third day was also in honor of the gods. The Cuzco people danced in long red robes, circling to the sad tones of the panpipes and flutes, which they loved more than any other music. Then flocks of pure white llamas suddenly invaded the great square. From the many thousands of them, the High Priest selected four; these were immediately killed and the bodies burnt before the gods.

The Inca then poured maize beer from an enormous gold-plated vase. This was very special chicha brewed from the whitest maize grown in the fields of Cuzco. The rest of the llamas were killed, skinned and roasted, and the whole population ate of this meat; it was a gift from the gods, because the white llamas were taken from the flocks belonging to the temples. Then the sick people and the unlucky ones were brought back to town and given their share of the meat and maize beer. It was a sign that the wealth of the community was to be given for the good of all, even the unfortunate.

The last day was one of colorful processions and dancing. Leaving their camps outside the city, the nations of Tahuantinsuyu marched in from the four directions. All were in tribal dress, led by their chiefs riding in befeathered litters, carried on the shoulders of their followers. Each tribe brought an image of its own god to the great square. There, with wild singing and dancing, the strange gods were presented to the gods of the Inca. The High Priest made the speeches of welcome, and then the images were taken away, each to its own little temple beside the Coricancha. The chiefs returned to the square with the old images which had been brought in at the previous year's Situa festival. The Inca then commanded them to be loaded with presents to take home.

It was a golden occasion of color and communal happiness. Cuzco was filled with brightness, and the singing and dancing went on all night. What was not wanted had been driven away; what was desired had been welcomed. Tahuantinsuyu had been strengthened, and the great gods honored.

terraces and towns

OUTSIDE CUZCO there were many beautiful towns and palaces. In the Valley of Yucay, the great Inca Tupac Yupanqui built himself a pleasure palace, of which a good deal of the stonework remains today. Among the curious things there, one can see the Inca's bath. It is a circular basin of stone into which a mountain spring pours a stream of fresh cold water. These Incas liked to take invigorating cold baths while they were staying in the green, moist valleys, away from the highland harshness of the Cuzco region. In those days the spring of water gushed through a silver tube, and the bath was lined with gold.

All this luxury was paid for by the work of the people. They filled the Inca's granaries with a third of their produce and gave the storehouses of the Sun still another third. The last third was for their own use. However, they gained very solid benefits in return for their high taxes; they were assured of peace and trade, of regular supplies of necessities in time of famine, and of entertainment and festivity at the great religious ceremonies. But each family had to produce three times the amount of food which would be needed for themselves. If they failed in this through their own fault, they went short. The supplies for the Sun and the Inca came before individual needs.

The consequence of all this organization was that every possible piece of land had to be cultivated. Towns and villages were built on bare rocky spurs of the mountains, so that no land should be wasted. The valleys were carefully irrigated and all fields had their share of the waters from the mountainsides. Then, when all the valleys were cultivated, the people extended their fields ever higher and higher until they reached the cold zones, where maize and quinoa could not be grown; even then, they managed to raise some potatoes. The grass of the high *puñas*, plateaus near the snow line, provided the pasturage for immense herds of llamas, where even the native herdsmen moved slowly because breathing was difficult. No land was wasted in ancient Peru.

The little fields up on the hillsides were called andenes; probably the name of the Andes came from them, just as in Europe the Alps are named from the alpen mountain pastures. The andenes on the mountainsides looked very like the vineyards of the Rhineland. At the foot of the slope a long wall of stones about two or three feet high was built by the villagers. The earth behind it was scraped down until it made a level shelf, reaching back from the wall. Then stones were collected and another wall built. Earth was again scraped down to make another level shelf. As soon as that was completed, another wall and shelf were begun; and so on, right up the mountainside, except where sheer precipices of bare rock barred the way.

Even the mountain streams were tamed. As they burst out of the rocks, or leapt over precipices, they were caught in stone basins and led into channels which ran along the walls. Running the length of one row of little fields, they turned and flowed through a stone gully into another channel along the lower level. So, before the stream reached the valley, it had spread its water wherever it was needed along the mountain fields.

Because of the need to build villages only on stony ground where crops were difficult to grow, it was usual for the village to stand above the fields which belonged to it. After the morning meal of maize porridge and herbs, the villagers would climb down the steep stairways of stones which led to their fields. There they would busy themselves caring for individual plants. They removed all weeds; absolutely nothing was left which might harm the development of the beloved maize. To the Incas, there was something sacred about the plant; it was more than an ordinary food crop.

They also grew quinoa, which is rather like millet with its great clusters of small seeds. On the walls of the fields they grew beans; and in the lower valleys, where it was warmer, they raised many kinds of pumpkins and gourds.

Potatoes were grown higher up the mountainsides, but with the same exact care with which maize was treated. They even made an occasional sacrifice of a human being to the potato spirits, but such killings were very rare in Peru. However, the strange way in which the potato could be cut up and a new plant

Terraced hillside for farming with stone walls bracing the many different levels.

grown from each "eye" was obviously a great proof of magic to them.

Many varieties of potatoes were grown in different soils and at different levels. One of the best was the small chuñu, which was grown on high ground. When harvested it was put in frost near the snow line. After freezing, the little white potatoes were crushed into a powder which could always be boiled in water to make a nourishing soup. The mountain villagers were not only desperately anxious to cultivate every inch of ground in their andenes, but they had a very good scientific knowledge of the crops they grew.

The usual village consisted of a row of stone-walled huts with thatched roofs and beaten clay floors. The stonework was rough—piled natural stones held together with clay. The doorposts and lintels were usually made of more carefully dressed stone. Archaeologically, such villages have left little more than their ground plan marked in heaps of rubble where the wall collapsed when the clay mortar was washed out.

These heaps were once simple one-roomed houses where most of the family property was kept in wooden chests. The bed was a boarded space lined with rugs. On the floor stood jars of water and drinking cups of wood and clay. Often there was a small stone-lined fire pit in the middle of the floor, in which charcoal was burned; it was safest to use charcoal, in view of the thick straw roofs.

Very often, cooking was done outside the hut in

big pottery vases supported on stones around a wood fire. There was always a special corner for the family digging-sticks, which were looked upon as sacred objects. Outside were a few stone-built granaries, with thatched lids. These held food stores, too—some for the Inca, some for the Sun, and some for the family.

Small villages were governed by headmen who ruled units of ten families, and were responsible for reporting to the Quipu-camayocs all cases of death, birth, and details of crop production. Few of them knew how to tie the knotted string quipus for themselves, but they usually knew enough to be able to see that the record was correct. The heads over ten families were directly responsible to heads of a hundred families. Each of these men usually kept a watchful eye over the welfare of several small mountain villages, reporting cases of need to the Inca nobles in the cities.

Sometimes serious outbreaks of illness demanded that food should be sent to aid the sick. Then the medical men from the towns would come with their herbal medicines and magical incantations to drive the illness away. Sometimes a landslide might sweep away fields on a mountainside, and it would be necessary to call for labor from the towns to rebuild the field walls. Such work was often performed by the soldiers of the town garrison.

Towns in the highlands were not very big. They were principally centers for the government officials, and places where markets were held, as well as the religious ceremonies at the new moon. At such times all the villagers flocked into them and enjoyed their day in a town well built of good stones. They met and exchanged goods; at one festival in the year they brought in all the young people who were to be married, and held a group wedding.

The regulation was that every young man of twenty-three or twenty-four who had finished his military service should marry. His bride was to be about eighteen or nineteen, and must be from the same tribe and district. That did not allow a very wide choice, but somehow the young people sorted themselves out and were married according to the law of the Incas.

The wedding festival was very gay. The Quipucamayoc tied the knots in his strings which recorded the number of households in each village. Then orders were given that a house should be built for each newly married couple, and that enough land on the andenes should be allotted to them for cultivation. When they left the town to return to their village, they felt no sense of being poor farm workers; they were first-class citizens of the Inca Empire, equal to anyone outside the Inca family.

To help them feel important and free, each new planting season was begun in Cuzco, where the Topa Inca and a line of the great nobles of the realm drove their digging-sticks of silver and gold and turned the first sods in the plantations of the Sun. To work and grow food was a gift from the Creator of all mankind, to Inca and hillside villager alike.

We are very fortunate that Peru possesses an almost complete country town of the Inca period. It was once well known, a fortress city above its fields, guarding a river gap which led through the wall of the Andes into the great forests of the Amazon basin. This was Macchu Pichu, visited by the Incas and later the refuge of the last heir to the Inca throne. The Spanish saw it at the time of the final moves in the war against the Incas. Eventually the town was deserted. There was no need for it as a fortress; and after the wars, and the pestilences which followed them, there was plenty of room for the people of Macchu Pichu to move down to the valleys where they could live and grow their food in greater comfort.

The town was abandoned. Trees grew from the grass in its streets. All was covered over and forgotten, except that the Indians preserved a tradition of the old city lost on a hilltop. Sometimes boys went hunting there, and climbed over the stone walls without being able to see that they were in an almost complete town, so thick was the mountaintop jungle.

It was in 1908 that Professor Hiram Bingham heard of this ruin high above the gorge of the Urubamba River. He climbed the precipitous rocks and crags into the forest. Sometimes there were sheer drops of nearly two thousand feet to the torrent below. Then, near the top of the crags, the stone walls began. They included passageways, square buildings, flights of steps, the rounded apse of a sun temple, then a clear space followed by a further group of walls on another crag. The first expedition succeeded in partially clearing the ancient town and making certain that Macchu Pichu was truly Inca. The pottery found here and there was typically Inca, and the buildings were quite like the remains of still finer palaces in Cuzco.

Two years later the site was fully surveyed and cleared. It provided few artifacts of any interest, but it did enable us to see an example of practical town planning in Inca times. There were andenes on all possible slopes below the town, and stone staircases ran through them, just wide enough for a loaded llama. The main entrances to the town had been cut through great boulders which made a natural fortress over the gateways. Between the houses the streets were narrow, with stone stairways wherever the trail became too steep for a level road.

The sun temple was in a commanding position at the edge of the plateau, with plenty of open space about it for ceremonial rites. At one side was a complete Intihuatana, a seat for the sun god. This circular enclosure centered around a short squared stone pillar with a step on one side—used to mark the days when the sun passed exactly overhead at noon. These occurred in February and October and were of importance to the priests, who were very good astronomers. To the ordinary people it was more important to observe the moon, because most of the festivals of their calendar were fixed by the lunar phases.

The buildings on the higher peak at Macchu Pichu included the fortress, with its walls arranged so that slingers and spear-throwers could strike downwards at an enemy; the walls were just a little too high for any enemy to leap up.

The buildings below the fortress may well have been the government offices of the town, but not a single knotted string quipu has survived the passing of time. This is a pity, because a group of quipus found together in one place might give some clue to the meaning of the colors used on the strings. Without that piece of knowledge, the quipus add up to numbers which have no meaning for us. However, the prevailing winds in this region come from the east, bringing wet clouds and fogs from the great forests of the Amazon basin, so it is too much to expect to find string records preserved as they have been in the dry sands of the desert coast of Peru.

Macchu Pichu must have been a key town in the system of fortresses which guarded the river valleys running down into the great forests of Antisuyu (the eastern region). Every now and again travelers discover one of these fortresses, built of carefully piled blocks of stone, on a clifftop overlooking the river valley. Such a place is the legendary city of Paititi, which remains almost inaccessible even in modern times.

But even beyond, in the fringes of the jungle itself, there were occasional stone-built outposts for Inca soldiers. These were dangerous places because of the devils which crept in silently at night and drove the soldiers mad with burning illnesses—at least, so the Peruvians described attacks of fever.

Moreover, the Indians of the forest were not always to be trusted. They came to trade beautiful bird feathers and jaguar skins for pottery and cloth, but these savages were suspicious and easily upset, and sometimes in their anger they would ambush and kill one or more of the Incas. Sometimes confederations of the forest tribes came up the river valleys to kill and burn mountain cities within the empire itself. So the defense system on the borders of the forest was very important and well planned: first the fringe of blockhouses, then the line of fortresses guarding each valley, and then the headquarters town with its narrow supply roads running out toward the frontier. Other roads ran inward toward the great highway of the Incas.

the road among the nations

EVER SINCE THE DISCOVERY of Peru by the Spaniards, the great roads of the Incas have been considered one of the wonders of the world.

It was easy enough to see that in order for the empire to expand there had to be good and safe roads so that the army could move rapidly from place to place. And the building of these roads involved some of the greatest feats of engineering ever contemplated by man. The main north-to-south highway was more than two thousand miles long. It climbed mountainsides by long stairways, tunneled through rocky spurs of the hills, edged along the sides of great precipices, leaped on swaying cable bridges across mile-deep ravines, and reached its distant goal safely.

Such a road would be a credit to any modern engineer with all the equipment of machines and explosives at our command today. The Inca engineers faced the problem with almost unlimited manpower armed with hammers, wedges, and levers of wood and bronze. If they wished to bore a tunnel they would light fires against the rock, and then throw cold water on the hot surfaces to make cracks into which the bronze levers could be inserted. In the worst places this fantastic road was five feet wide; on good safe ground it was twenty feet wide.

Every time the Inca frontiers were expanded, the roads were continued through the new territories. The armies were made up mainly of ordinary young men kept from two to five years on duty, but there must have been a very highly skilled group of specialists to direct the road-building work. The great swinging bridges over mountain ravines could not have been designed by the local villagers. Later on they would be responsible for replacing the cables of twisted osier twigs which held up the roadway, but the construction of a span that would support the passage of an army or a thousand loaded llamas could only be the work of experts.

First the route had to be surveyed. The bridge must be placed at a spot where the two banks were level with each other, and where the approaches of the road could be made safely. Once this was arranged for, holes big enough for a man to crawl through were cut

An Inca swinging bridge over a mountain ravine.

in the solid rock. These were the eyelets through which
the cables of the bridge would pass. If there was no
suitable rock available in the selected place, the builders would prepare the eyelets in a large block of stone
and then anchor it by erecting a massive pyramid of
heavy blocks above it to hold it in position.

When the anchorages on both sides of the ravine
had been made secure, lead-men would clamber down
the steep banks with a thin strong cotton rope. They
would throw it down from one level ledge to the next
until they came to the river, perhaps a mile below the
bridge. Now bravery was needed. One was likely to

be swept away by the torrent and smashed to pulp among the rocks, but the cable had to be taken across. Men would leap from rock to rock, or try to swim from pool to pool across the river, aided as soon as possible by a string thrown from the party on the other side. They themselves carried a string tied to the end of the long rope. Once over, the team of men to whom they handed their string would start heaving on it until they had brought the end of the rope safely across. All the time the men on the other side who had taken the rope down were easing its passage so that it would not tear on the rocks. As its end passed over the river it was tied with a strong cord let down from above, and slowly drawn up from level to level by teams of men.

Meanwhile the main cables for the bridge had been prepared from osier twigs, long and pliant, woven together into a gigantic cord some ten inches across and perhaps two hundred yards long. One end of a cable was passed through the stone eyelet in the anchorage and bound secure. The other end was fixed to the cotton rope. Gradually by means of pulling and adjusting the rope and then the cable fastened to it, the massive strand was hauled across the abyss and fastened on the other side. The cable was never pulled taut because the Peruvians knew well enough that changes in the weather might make it shrink, especially as the twigs coiled up more tightly when wet. So to make sure that it could not break, they let it hang over the ravine in a graceful shallow curve.

Now all was ready for the next cable to be brought over. The Peruvian mountaineers had no fear of heights; a group of them would take the rope on their shoulders and walk over the single cable. The only preparation they made was to leave their sandals behind. They walked smartly down the curve and then up the other side with their rope.

Once again the tug-of-war began, and the second big cable was taken over. This had to be more carefully adjusted at the far end, to lie exactly alongside the first one. Two or three more big cables were pulled over and secured. Next, about three feet higher, a lighter cable was placed on either side to act as a handrail, laced by cords to the main cables so that it was always within easy reach of the footway.

The last thing done was to lay the footway of short lengths of boards running across the width of the cables. The bridges varied in width according to the importance of the road. But even two centuries after the Spanish Conquest many of them remained strong enough to bear the weight of a heavy stagecoach.

Thus the Incas made it possible to pass rapidly from one spot to another within the empire. Food, supplies, armies, could all be moved easily and efficiently.

Down in the coastlands the ancient civilizations had also built local road systems, but the Incas made these into one unified roadway along the whole length of the coast. It was almost as difficult to build as the mountain highway, but for different reasons. The shallow river valleys had to be crossed by simple stone slab bridges and steppingstones; the sandy drifts of the desert coast had to be swept clear from the fixed route, which was marked by great tree trunks set in straight lines beside the trail. But such difficulties were faced by the Inca engineers as a problem to be solved for the honor of the sun god. There was no such word as "impossible"; they just went on with the work until they had succeeded.

We owe a great deal of our knowledge of the remains of the great coastal highway of the Incas to the archaeologist Victor von Hagen, who took the trouble to go and look for all signs of the route between the few well-known sections. He succeeded in tracing almost the whole of it. Then he followed up the clues of fragments of roads, the places of ancient ruins, and records in the old chronicles. It was a matter of great patience and exact weighing of all the evidence, but in the end almost the whole of the Inca road system has been made clear to us.

It was far more than the two great highways; it was a network of crossing roads linking cities with one another, and making the natural paths of the river valleys easier for travelers. It brought the centers of the country districts into the network of main roads, and to them it led the smaller roads and mountain trails from the farming villages and the high pastures of the llama breeders. In fact, the road system was as organic as the veins in a leaf, taking nourishment from one part to another. In some ways it was an even better-planned system than the Roman road network.

It was only after the discovery of the real complexity of the network of Inca roads that the stories told by the conquerors about the many millions of Indians in the Inca Empire seemed to become living facts. After the conquest, many plagues had swept the country. Since the Indians had almost no resistance to the diseases of Europe, the population was halved in the generation after the conquest. Then people settled in new areas, where the colonial government found employment for them at the seaports and near the rich mines of silver and gold. The ancient road system fell into disuse after a few years, and only the great main roads were kept open. The Spaniards had horses and donkeys, so the roads were not so necessary as they had been in Inca days when all traffic had been on foot.

In the highlands the Indians retired into themselves, keeping apart from the white men as far as they could. They farmed only for their own needs, and did not use the ancient roads for carrying supplies for the Sun and the Inca. Everything was changed to such a degree that only the patient work of an archaeologist traveling along the ancient pathways could reveal the colorful and crowded past as it had really existed.

In olden times the great valleys of Peru were fringed by small towns and villages all the way up to the mountain plateaus. Every two or three miles along the roads were rest houses for messengers, and stores of food and clothing for distribution to the army or people in distressed areas. The roads were not empty stretches between towns, but were constantly busy in the easygoing Peruvian way. Llamas could not be hurried, and they were the real means of transport. Every mile or two the llama convoys would decide to sit down, and there was no moving them until they felt ready. When the leading llama, who wore bells on his harness, would rise tinklingly to his feet, all the others would do the same. The Indian drover in his bright tunic and colored headband would roll himself another pellet of coca leaves from his wallet, and as he started to chew he would shuffle his tired feet into his sandals and move along at a steady jogtrot beside his llamas for another short stage.

A llama could only carry about seventy pounds, so there were many of them in a big convoy of goods. They were used for carrying bales of cloth, wooden boxes, pottery, bundles of foodstuffs, and so on, from one town to another. They brought the farmer's goods to the market, and his taxes to the storehouses of the Inca and the Sun.

Other road users were the Chasquis, who ran with messages from one town to another, or to Cuzco with news and valuables for the Inca. These were highly trained runners who would travel at top speed for about two miles till they reached a rest house. Then their packet or message would be handed over to another runner who would set off on his own two-mile course. There was no break in this relay service, and among other things it enabled the Inca in the mountains to eat fresh fish which had been caught in the ocean on the preceding day. He could receive a knotted quipu telling of events a thousand miles away, and that within three days of their happening. By such means the central government at Cuzco kept in constant touch with all the empire. Of course news of expected events could be sent more quickly by means of smoke signals from selected hilltops by day and beacons of fire by night. Indians in our own United States used this system. However, the Peruvian Chasquis carrying their knotted string records were the equivalent of dispatch riders everywhere.

The most brilliant sight on the roads of Inca Peru was the cortege of an Inca when traveling. First would come squadrons of soldiers in the checkerboard-patterned quilted tunics and polished copper helmets with fringes of feathers. Then came groups of officials, carried in litters supported on the shoulders of runners. These officials would be gorgeously dressed with badges of their office decorating their headdresses. Their runners would wear special uniforms. Then, with a guard of red-dressed warriors and runners of noble birth with bright tunics and great golden ear-discs, would come the Inca himself, riding in a brightly colored and gilded throne under an umbrella of colored feathers. The throne would be supported on long poles with eight runners at each side. If a runner slipped he would be replaced by another, and then killed; there was no room for inefficiency or accident in the service of the Inca.

Following the throne would come more officials and the ladies of the court riding in covered litters. These in turn would be followed by servants carrying loads of cloth and bundles of specially selected presents for the cities which the Inca was going to visit. The whole cortege would pass along at a steady jogtrot of about five miles an hour. No Peruvians would walk on a journey. They found it easier to keep up an even trot. As the cortege passed toward a village or town, people

An Inca official riding in his litter borne by runners and accompanied by soldiers in uniform.

would rush out to line the streets and call out blessings on the Inca, but as soon as he came in sight they would become silent and throw themselves on the ground, not daring to look up to see the face of the Child of the Sun.

The people met the Inca face to face only when he was safely installed in one of their towns. Then there would be ceremonies and much feasting from the stores reserved for his use. Presents would be given to the governor of the town, and special gifts of local workmanship would be brought to delight the Inca. Then the people could flock into the square before the Inca's throne to perform the dances and sing the traditional songs of their tribe.

There were few surprises for the Inca in any Peruvian town. He knew all about the national costumes of the people from their dress at the festivals in Cuzco. As for the towns, he had exactly carved relief maps which showed the size and position of every building in them. It was policy to make these tours, because the people of recently conquered tribes saw that the Inca was not unwilling to stay among them, and that he really treated them as full citizens of the empire. It was a great factor for unity. They also felt very happy because he did not try to interfere much with their local way of life.

Only people who had official business with the Inca authorities needed to learn the Quechua language. The gods of the tribes were respected, and were even housed in the little temples around the Coricancha in Cuzco. Only on certain festivals the Inca's governor led the people in the worship of Inti, the sun god. Nobody was allowed to wear gold any more unless he had been adopted into the Inca family at least by marriage; but in any case only a few nobles in any province had been able to wear gold. In most cases the provincial nobles still retained their offices, and the chief himself was confirmed in his position and often married to an Inca lady. The whole business of government under the Incas was made as friendly and easy as possible. That was not only the most sensible way, but also the cheapest in manpower.

It was always easy for the Inca to know if anyone was plotting against him, because there were Inca officials in every city of the empire. Also every different tribe wore its national costume with a distinctive headdress. If the officials noticed an unusual gathering of people from different tribes, they immediately began to look for the reason. It might be nothing more serious than arranging for a festival display of dances; but, on the other hand, it was impossible for any single tribe to hope to overthrow the Inca power, so meetings between different tribes *might* indicate a plot.

Sometimes there was indeed a plot, and an actual revolt. This was usually due to some foolish oppression by an Inca governor. Perhaps the revolt reached the point where a citadel was stormed and a governor killed. In such a case the Inca army moved in. If the

84

rebellious tribesmen surrendered quickly they were often pardoned, but the tribe would be divided. According to the law, the Inca could move his subjects to any part of the empire just as he wished.

The law about deportees was very wisely planned. No person from the hot lands was to be sent to the high cold lands, and no highlander was sent to a hot climate. Each one was placed where he could live in the way he was used to. Families were not broken up, and in the new settlement they were given as much land as they had held before.

The usual thing was to send people who had been obedient and friendly to live among tribes which were unfriendly, and to bring some of the unfriendly tribespeople to live among the more settled peoples. Such colonists were called mitimaes, and they were treated with kindness. For the first two years of their exile they were exempted from all taxes so that they could make their living more easily while they settled down in their new homes. Nobody pretended that it was a good thing to be taken from one's familiar mountain valley and sent to a place hundreds of miles away, but in time the new valley became "home" and the settled villagers happily paid their taxes again to the Inca and the Sun.

The people who had wanted to revolt heard all about the benefits of the Inca rule from the more settled people who were now living among them. The empire was just that little bit more united and at peace. Yet the two tribal groups remained separate, and were made to keep their distinctive tribal dress. The Incas had not yet discovered the Roman idea of gradually making all subject tribes part of one imperial nation. But wherever they were, the leaders of each group of a tribe were made responsible to the Inca governor. There was no attempt to do anything more than replace a hostile leader with a friendly one from the same family. In fact, the Inca policy in these matters was more humane than anything the world can show today.

One of the most difficult of all problems faced by the Inca government was the protection of public health. Epidemics were watched, and movement of people and llamas into and out of the danger area was restricted. There was no sewage system in the towns, but each household kept its sewage in big covered jars, and their contents were taken out for use as manure in the fields. Among the villagers the same was done; the sewage used as fertilizer was dug into the ground day by day, and thus never became a nuisance or cause of disease.

The Inca system included a rudimentary medical service with its specialists in setting broken limbs and trepanning skulls and so on. But most doctors were simply people who were interested enough to learn about the properties of herbs and how to use them to help their neighbors. They received presents of food and cloth to make up for the time they spent while acting as doctors. There were always women in towns and villages who specialized as midwives, and who were not only rewarded with presents but also had a small extra allowance of cloth and foodstuffs from the Inca's stores. It was all very well organized, like everything which the Incas took in hand.

The one tragic mistake which brought about the fall of the Inca Empire was made by the eleventh Topa Inca, the great and brave Huayna Capac. He had conquered the kingdom of Quito, and for the first time brought the Inca Empire to the equator and a little north of it.

To seal the conquest with friendship in the traditional way, the Inca married the daughter of the Scyri of Quito. He had the unusual misfortune to fall in love with this lady. Huascar, his son by the Coya, was the true heir to the throne; but by the beautiful princess of Quito he had another son, Atahuallpa. Huayna Capac thought that it was possible to divide the empire. He planned to have Huascar succeed him as Topa Inca, and to give Atahuallpa a separate kingdom of Quito, with an equal rank as supreme Inca. No doubt he had forgotten the prophecy that linked the Incas with the succession of the twelve moons of the year. Huascar was to be the twelfth and last Topa Inca.

After the death of Huayna Capac, Topa Inca Huascar was placed on his throne, and he was unwise enough to let his half brother live. Atahuallpa set to work to seize his part of the inheritance, with the help of two Peruvian generals, Quizquiz and Chalcuchima.

He managed to hold off the Topa Inca, and then in a sharp campaign spread through four years he achieved control of the whole country. He seized Huascar, and had himself acknowledged as true Inca by the High Priest. At this juncture the Spaniards landed. Atahuallpa took this opportunity to remove all internal opposition by having Huascar murdered.

Due to the treachery of Quizquiz and Chalcuchima, the country was left without an Inca; the system had collapsed. The twelve Incas had reigned for nearly five centuries. The false Atahuallpa was captured and killed. The Spaniards, learning of the true state of affairs, hunted down the two princes who could have claimed the rights to become Topa Inca and killed them. After that, the members of the Inca family no longer presented a danger to their conquerors, and a number of them, including the father of Guaman Poma de Ayala, were ennobled with Spanish titles which made them grandees under the new empire of Spain.

As it was with the Inca roads, so it was with the political organization: once the Topa Inca was gone, the whole elaborate system fell into ruin.

fishers of the great ocean

ONE OF THE most remarkable feats of Inca organization was the successful holding of the people of the Chimu kingdom within the Inca Empire. The Incas and the highland people in general detested the rich, luxury-loving lowlanders. Still more they disliked the climate. They found it made them as lazy in the heat of the day as any Chimu prince might be. Moreover, the air pressure near sea level together with the high temperatures and extremely dry air gave them headaches and sore throats. Yet in spite of this, they kept their officials in all important towns, and won the respect of the lowlanders.

For one thing the Incas arranged to join in the worship of the creator sea god Pachacamac, by making it

89

quite clear that he was in fact their own great creator Viracocha. They made offerings at his temple, and often paid state visits. The heart of the Chimu kingdom long resisted them; but, by careful bribery and friendly conduct to the Chimu chief and his gods, the Incas were able to hold their position as overlords.

The capture of the Chimu kingdom was made by the Topa Inca Tupac Yupanqui, who was one of the greatest organizers of the Inca Empire. It is said that he was so bold that he went on a sea voyage by balsa rafts, and after visiting some strange islands in the great ocean returned home nearly half a year later.

Chimu fishermen in a reed boat.

There is no reason to doubt the story, because Tupac Yupanqui could well leave the government in the capable hands of his son Huayna Capac. Only recently the explorer-archaeologist Thor Heyerdahl proved that a small balsa raft made in the ancient way could be navigated from Lima in Peru across the Pacific as far as the Tuamotu Islands. The people of the Marquesas Islands also had a tradition that their ancestors had once made a great sailing canoe which had visited a mountainous continent and safely returned across the Pacific to their home.

Most of the Chimu people were fishermen. They built fine towns, and irrigated fields near the river mouths of their desert coastlands; but, naturally, they were forced to rely mostly on the sea. The great South Pacific current of cool water swept northward along the coast of Peru, bringing an almost inexhaustible supply of fish of all kinds, from giant rays and sharks to masses of little fish not unlike sardines. These fish were preyed on by innumerable sea lions who lived among the rocks and cliffs, where ridges of stone ran down into the ocean. There were pelicans and cormorants and gulls, which made the rocks white with deposits of guano. The sea edge swarmed with crabs and all kinds of shellfish.

This was a rich world for fishermen. Yet they were tormented by the sun. In the heat of the day, the desert coast shimmered in the heat haze, and people hid from it in whatever shelter they could find. No wonder they could not understand the Incas who worshiped this terrible celestial body. When at midday Cuzco was busy with activity, the Chimu capital Chan Chan was silent in the heat; a silver haze softened the brilliant frescoes of the mud-brick houses, and people lay resting and longing for a breath of cool air. Chan Chan awoke for business in the late afternoon, and many people worked by moonlight or the smoky glow of tight-bound reed torches. Wood was too scarce to burn.

Chimu houses were simple courtyards like those of the Incas, but built of sun-dried brick. The roofs were of reed thatch, held in place by a few twisted wooden supports from the small trees which grew on the fringe of the cultivated river valleys. Poorer people often lived in huts made of reed mats stretched round a simple wooden frame.

When the Incas marched in, they found fortresses made in terraced mounds like their own, but these were not built from stone. Instead, a natural rising ground of rock was covered by tons of brick facings to give it the necessary shape and strength. It was the same with the temples. No fine stone constructions like the Coricancha were to be found in the whole of the coastlands. Instead the temples were step pyramids of brick. One great brick mound stood on another; there were usually six or seven stages, not very high or steep, but adding up to a hundred feet or so. Up one face ran a broad stairway to the sanctuary on top. All the faces of the pyramid were covered with a lime cement which was painted in gay colors with symbols of the gods. Then at the top came the holy house of the god, usually a little mud-brick hovel with a cane-matting roof.

The Inca was horrified when one of the great gods was shown to him. Instead of a glittering figure of gold or even porphyry, the divine image was a crude wooden post carved with a simple face rubbed over with red paint. That it was already more than a thousand years old did not matter to the Inca; he felt it was a sad strange thing that the images of the gods should be made from so ordinary a material.

The great festivals of the coast people were, however, very brilliant and gay. They used more feathers than the highlanders, and were skilled in working silver and gold, so that everyone could appear in glittering metal ornaments. Some wore shirts covered with little fish made out of sheets of silver. Others had little moons and circular discs of alternate silver and gold. Their ear ornaments and cloak pins were shaped in openwork filigree to give elegance and glitter. On such occasions the image of the god was wrapped in feathered robes and brought down the steps by the priests to be enthroned among the people, who danced and sang in his honor. True, he was an ancient oracle; but they were singing the praises of the bringer of fish, the giver of sea lions, the breath of life on the waters. Somehow it was much more primitive than an Inca festival, but it was also much more free and happy. The god was part of the nation, and not a great outside force.

Perhaps the Inca invaders received their greatest shock at the spring festivals, when the young people came out at sunrise. No one wore a scrap of clothing, and as the sun tipped the horizon they ran in one wild scramble to get to the temple steps. Scrambling up the steep slope toward the temple, they sorted themselves out into pairs, and the boy and girl who first reached the house of the god hand-in-hand were supposed to bring blessings on the people. They were honored as priest and priestess of the growing crops, and married there and then.

To the Chimu, this was a wonderful thing which symbolized the union of human beings with the whole of Nature, and all youth with the springtime. But the Incas were not attuned to nudism in their gray plateau among the clouds, and their gods were very stern and splendid beings; so they did not attend such festivals of the lowlanders, even though they were unable to stop them.

Even the llamas of the Inca homeland could not live long in the hot coastal countries. Air pressure was high, and the heat and dryness killed the poor animals. So nearly all the traffic on the great Inca highway through the sands was carried on the backs of men and women. On morning and evening journeys the convoys of porters trotted along the roads, supporting their bundles by a tumpline round their foreheads, just as the highland people did. Everything was carried in this way, from bundles of raw cotton to large jars full of the local drinks. Notables, of course, were carried about in their fine litters, like the Inca noblemen at home.

One of the real charms of the coast for the Inca was the delicate fish food. The Chasquis used to send fish by relay race up to Cuzco, and the Inca enjoyed it as a particular treat from the richest and strangest province of his empire.

The Chimu people used many methods in fishing. No doubt much of their skill was traditional. People had been fishing with hook and line from that coast for at least four thousand years. We have plenty of pictures of Chimu fishermen from the molded pots which they left behind in their graves. We see them seated in their little boats made up of two or three big bundles of totora reeds tied together. Over the side they lower their hooks on a string without a rod. Sometimes they hook a shark as big as their boat, sometimes a more peaceful flatfish.

These dawn-and-dusk fishing trips must have been quite pleasant occasions while the weather was fine, but in storms there was danger of the little reed boats being driven out to sea where they could become waterlogged and lost. One could not take such a boat out for many hours at a time without having to hurry home to dry it out before going off again.

Some fishermen seem to have made themselves little huts out of several of these reed boats, with the thick ends standing on the ground and the narrow prows curving over to form a pointed roof.

The Chimu kings were the heads of a very rich community. Their traders took all manner of goods up and down the coasts of Peru and Ecuador. It was quicker to carry a big load on a balsa raft from one port to another than to send the same amount of goods in bundles on the backs of hundreds of porters; it was cooler, too, to travel on the sea.

Many of the great trading balsas were ships of considerable size. Among the first Peruvian vessels met by the Spanish invaders was a trading balsa going along the coast of Ecuador with a cargo of cotton, pottery, silver and gold vessels, jars of chicha drink, and bundles of woven cloth. The crew of forty men and women included a merchant and his carriers. Though it rode low in the water, it was as big as any of the little ships which Pizarro had been able to obtain for his great adventure.

A balsa raft was a very cleverly worked-out vessel. It could be adjusted to any size by adding or removing extra side timbers. If treated properly it would float for a year or more before it became so waterlogged that it had to be taken ashore for drying out.

This business of becoming waterlogged had long been a problem for archaeologists. Acquaintance with the light dry balsa wood gave the impression that it would become waterlogged very quickly, and there was absolutely no record of any special treatment of the timbers and no evidence of them having been painted over with waterproof mastic or anything else.

The problem was solved in 1947 by Thor Heyerdahl, who, wishing to build a balsa raft for himself, experimented with fresh logs still containing the natural sap of the trees. They were a little heavier than dry balsa wood, but they remained free of sea water over the whole of his long voyage.

The first step in building a balsa raft was to prospect very carefully to find a group of trees all about the same height and thickness. The raft-builders cut them down with their small bronze axes. The wood was soft and did not blunt the soft edges of the axe-blades. The fallen trees were not left to season, but were quickly stripped of branches and bark. They were then carried down to the workshops near the sea where the craft would be constructed.

The logs were arranged with the butt ends together and the tops closed a little, to make a kind of prow to the raft. They were tied together loosely with cane ties, leaving slight spaces between the logs. By this means the raft was made flexible, so that it could bend a little when riding heavy waves. It also allowed water to splash in and out between the balsa trunks, so that the raft was never filled with water. Across the trunks two beams of wood were laid, tied only at the end. On them a platform of light planks was placed, supporting a cabin covered with mats. In this way the cabin floor was kept fairly dry above the waterline. The purpose

Balsa raft with cabin and square sail. Inca rafts like these were able to navigate five hundred miles out to sea.

of the cabin was to give shelter to passengers, as well as to protect perishable merchandise. Other goods, such as bundles of pottery and sealed boxes, were piled near the middle trunk of balsa wood. On the outer logs were pegs holding a rope to support the members of the crew when they sat there to propel the great raft with six-foot-long wooden paddles.

Near the middle of the sides of the raft two long poles were set up, which crossed at about twice a man's height above the deck. From the crossing a yardarm holding a square sail was slung. Guy ropes held the double mast in position, and there were other ropes to veer the sail round to catch the winds. This was a

Peruvian invention, and the only sail used in the whole of the South American continent.

The balsa raft rode only on the surface of the sea. It was therefore at the mercy of the winds unless there was some way to guide it, so the Peruvians worked out a system of "center-board" steering. Center-boards were planks about the height of a man, and nine inches broad, about an inch thick at the back and tapered to a thin edge along the front. At the top was a carved handle. Ten or twelve of these boards were pushed between the logs of the raft.

When they were all up, the balsa would skim across the waves with the wind and even go sideways. When the boards at the back were pushed down, they steadied the course of the vessel so that a wind coming from the side could still be used to drive the ship forward, and not push it lightly across the water in the wrong direction. One could also adjust the center-boards fore and aft so that the ship could be turned, either into the wind or to run before it. By this means the Peruvian navigators were able to guide the apparently clumsy rafts up and down the long coastline.

It was only in 1953 that careful excavations were made in the Galapagos Islands by Thor Heyerdahl and his companions. They found a number of ancient Peruvian pottery vessels, mostly from Inca times but a few from a thousand years earlier. It seems evident that the ancient balsas were able to navigate five hundred miles out to sea without any great difficulty. Heyerdahl's

Kon-Tiki voyage of three thousand miles to the Tua-motu Islands was final proof of the seaworthiness of the balsa. It had long been known that there were native traditions in this part of Polynesia about a great king who came on rafts with many people from the west; it may be that this referred to the famous voyage of the Inca Tupac Yupanqui, but so far no archaeological proof has been found.

If the *Kon-Tiki* raft had sailed from the North Peruvian port of Tumbez, where Pizarro first landed on the mainland, the journey would have brought the raft to the Marquesas Islands. It is from the Marquesas that we have the ancient story of the giant canoe which was launched seventy generations ago to sail to the land of Tefiti, which was almost certainly the mainland of South America. The probable date of this journey would be about 900 A.D., before the time of the Incas. The Marquesan story as recorded by Handy in 1923 is so circumstantial that it is hard to find any explanation except that Polynesian voyagers really visited Peru. Thus it seems certain that the remarkable voyage attributed to Tupac Yupanqui was at least a possibility.

It is probable that on some such voyage across the oceans the Peruvians introduced the sweet potato into the islands of Polynesia. Whether they were responsible for introducing to the native peoples of Formosa the center-board method of steering bamboo rafts is a matter for conjecture. It may well have been that a balsa raft was taken there by a Spanish ship in the sixteenth century. We have no record to show when the Formosan tribes first used this method of navigation.

Nor is there evidence of any Peruvian balsas having traveled north of Ecuador. When Pizarro and his associates Almagro and Padre Luque met in Panama, they heard native stories about a wonderful land of gold far to the south; however, they could find no one who had traveled there, and they saw nothing which was said to have come from that mysterious southern land. Later on, when Pizarro touched at the coast, he found only swamps and wild jungle as far as the island of Gallo. He found several villages of Indians who wore a few ornaments of gold, but they had only small canoes, and were in no sense civilized.

It seems clear that these long desolate coasts of tropical rain forest discouraged the Peruvian navigators from searching for trade in that direction. To the south they penetrated to the coast of central Chile, but that was only with the advance of the Inca armies into this almost empty desert.

Inca travel inland does not seem to have left any traces north of Ecuador. As we know, they were in contact with the wild tribes of the Amazon forest, but there is no evidence that they attempted to explore the river valleys. Farther south, Inca fortresses were constantly on the alert against invasions by the Diaguita confederacy of tribes in northwest Argentina. These people built small towns of stone houses, and made very good bronze weapons, as well as fine pottery which often imitates Inca styles. They were great warriors, and having captured a young Spaniard from a ship in the La Plata estuary, they carried him on a raid into the Inca Empire before it was discovered by Pizarro. It is said that these Diaguitas introduced the domestic fowl into Peru, but it seems more likely that this bird arrived here some centuries earlier across the Pacific.

If the Inca Empire had not fallen to Pizarro, there were only two lines of expansion open to the Peruvians. Probably they would have moved southward and absorbed the Diaguita, and this would have opened up the Pampas of Argentina with their almost inexhaustible flocks of guanacos, as well as the open parkland of the Paraguayan Chaco. This was not densely populated country and would have served as a reservoir to take the crowded population from parts of Peru itself,

In the north, after the fatal conquest of Ecuador, the Peruvians would have found an easy mountain way to the rich gold valley of the Cauca River in Colombia, and to the great plateaus near Bogotá where the empire of the Chibcha had its center. We know that the Chibcha raided as far afield as British Guiana, so we need have no doubt that the Incas could have reached the shores of the Caribbean.

However, this was not to be. The fatal mistake of Inca Huayna Capac led to the sealing off of the empire in Ecuador, and its division, in the very year in which Pizarro landed. If the empire had remained united it may well be that Pizarro would have been defeated and killed, but there is no doubt that Spanish adventurers would have come pressing upon the country from the north, where they had captured the Chibcha Empire, as well as from the south, where they had entered Paraguay. The Pacific would have been filled with adventurers seeking their share of the gold. Whatever happened, the Inca Empire was doomed. It is perhaps less tragic that the last true Topa Inca was murdered by his half brother shortly after the arrival of the invaders from the sea.

knotted strings
and painted boards

AFTER THE fall of Peru, the Spaniards needed to know what was produced by the people of the country which they had captured so suddenly. Most of these men were soldiers with no knowledge of how to organize a government. They tried to keep part of the old system, so they took their records down on paper from the dictation of the Quipu-camayocs who interpreted the knotted strings. Some of the Spaniards have left us accounts of how numbers could be read from the strings, but not one has told us clearly how to understand what was meant by the colors of these quipus.

It is even worse with the other kind of Peruvian records, the painted wooden boards. Guaman Poma de Ayala tells us that, as a child, he saw the painted boards on which were depicted the history of each Inca, but these boards are completely lost to us, though we know that they were probably very much like the wooden beakers called keros, of which a few specimens still survive. These keros are often decorated with human figures and patterns, made with mastic.

Mastic is a natural gum drawn from a bush; it is a clear liquid and dries by contact with the oxygen in the air in exactly the same way as the more delicate Chinese lacquer. This mastic could be mixed into a paste with mineral powders of any color. The colored paste was pressed into hollows cut in the wood-work, smoothed down and allowed to dry. When every part of the pattern had been filled with its appropriate color and dried, the whole vessel was polished over with fine sand and leaves to make it smooth and glossy. Such a vessel was very beautiful, a treasured possession in the home.

In ancient times these keros were used for pouring out offerings of drink to the gods. Today, after four centuries, their colors are still distinct, though often dimmed by the dirt from many generations of human hands. If only the boards had been preserved like the keros, how valuable they would be in revealing to us the records described by Guaman Poma. But not one of them is known to exist today. Perhaps in some museum or old castle in Spain, Austria, or Italy a board may be found remaining from the treasures of Peru which were sent to the Hapsburg Emperors.

We have many of the string quipus, however. All come from the coasts, where they were buried in the dry sand with their former owners. Not a single one comes from the highland homes of the Incas.

At first sight they look like jumbled masses of knitting wool. They have to be carefully spread out, and then it is seen that they are made of a top string of colored cotton, from which finer strings hang down. Each of these finer strings is tied into knots at several different levels. Each knot is made of a number of turns of string around the central cord. The turns vary in number from one to ten, so confirming the Spanish account of the quipus which insists that a decimal system was used by the Incas. It appears that the knots nearest to the main string are the units, the second row of knots are the tens, the third are hundreds, and the fourth are thousands. Sometimes the smaller strings are of different colors and obviously deal with special parts of the account, but we have no means of knowing what they actually mean.

The only quipus which have been actually translated are two in Paris which were analyzed by the late Baron Erland Nordenskiöld. They recorded the apparent movements of the moon and Venus, so that we can be sure that Peruvian astronomers were good at their work. Of course they had no real thought for people so different from themselves as we are; their intention was to leave an accurate record of their observations for their own race.

They were thoroughly scientific in their careful and patient routine recording of what they saw in the sky. It was quite clear to them that the records of a thousand years might be required to check off the movements of the planets so well that they could predict exactly which planets would be visible in the sky on any given night.

They were also able to predict eclipses of the sun and moon, so they must have kept a very good record of these events to find the rhythm of time in which the eclipses could occur. To record such long mathematical calculations, the quipus were ideal. Each detail could be counted up exactly in its place, and added to the next step of calculation on the following string.

The quipus which have come down to us are from the coast, and some of them date from five or six centuries before the Incas came to Cuzco. This proves that schoolboys in Peru were tying their sums in knots long before the Incas organized a school system.

There was indeed a school system in Inca Peru. Just as girls were sent to the House of the Virgins of the Sun, boys were selected and sent to schools where they were taught the mysteries of the quipus by wise elders. Of course, all boys of Inca blood received this schooling, because their position in the Inca state demanded that they should understand how records were kept and how the government of the country had grown. But the Incas depended so much upon the record system that many thousands of other boys were trained

The monolithic Intihuatana sun throne in the hill city of Macchu Pichu. This pillar was used for calculating dates.

as civil servants, who would have the responsibility for seeing literally that no knot was left untied in the strings of government.

Father Calancha has left us a record of one school exercise in historical quipus: "Record the following history. There had been nothing before the first Inca Manco Capac. In his reign in the fourth year he captured ten provinces, killing many enemies and losing three thousand of his own soldiers. He gained ten thousand handfuls of gold and thirty thousand of silver."

From the rather confused account which follows, we see that a black cord represented time. To this were tied some unbleached cords scattered with irregular knots. (Time was passing; nothing important was recorded, and numbers were uncertain.) Next would come a red knot. (The Inca: one guesses that since this was the first red cord it meant the first Inca, Manco Capac.) In the red cord a knot of four turns would be made. (Year four of the first Inca.) To the last knot a brown thread would be fixed with a knot of ten turns. (Ten earth districts added in the fourth year of the first Inca.)

Then Father Calancha goes on to say that to the brown knots green cords were added, but no quipu is known with so many off-branches. It may well be that we should have returned to the black cord of passing time. The green cords were added next. ("Many enemies" would be expressed by a number of scattered small knots without placing.)

Then Inca troops killed. We are not given a color clue here, so we guess: red for the Inca and white for dead men's bones, so a red-and-white cord is added close to the green one, with no knot in the units place, no knot in the tens, no knot in the hundreds, but a knot of three turns in the thousands place. (Three thousand Inca men dead.) The captured silver was a white cord (a triple knot in the ten thousands place); the gold was possibly a yellow cord (one knot in the ten thousands place). We now have a problem: a festival day was declared for the Sun. (We guess again: Sun, gold, Inca, red; one knot in a red-and-gold cord on the time cord.) But maybe, as in some real quipus, it mattered a good deal whether the lesser cords were above or below the main cord.

School life in Inca days was not easy. The children were responsible for the cleaning of the school, and life was made as hard as possible for them so that they should be able to face difficulties more bravely in later life. One gains the impression that a great deal of learning came simply through fear of the lash of the master.

For the richer pupils, those of Inca blood, the training was conducted by a special class of wise old men. These tutors directed the entire life of their pupils, giving them wise advice and teaching them the ancient wisdom of the kings and priests. They even acted as judges of their pupils' progress in the great examination of their ability as skilled warriors.

This examination was something like a modern train-

111

ing course for commandos. It took place in the year when the candidate was sixteen, and lasted from one new moon till the next. The young men had to show their strength in wrestling and running. There were fights with shields and clubs, and though the clubs had no stone or bronze mace heads on them, they were still dangerous enough to kill if one received an unlucky blow. The most difficult ordeals were five-day journeys made without food. The candidates wore only coarse tunics, and were allowed neither sandals nor bedding.

There was no easy way to become a warrior; the

Sixteen-year-old boys fighting with shields and clubs as part of their warriors' examination.

whole course had to be passed to the satisfaction of the tutors. If a boy failed, it was a worse disgrace than if he had been killed in a mock combat. So strictly fair were the judges of this ordeal that only once was the heir of a reigning Inca chosen as the best of all the candidates in the examination. This was the great Tupac Yupanqui.

After passing their ordeal the young men were washed and dressed in white. They were brought before the Inca, who made a long speech and then commanded them to come to him one by one. As they knelt at his knees the Topa Inca pierced each of his ears with a golden pin. This was allowed to remain, a sign that they were accepted as good members of the Inca family. Little by little the holes in the ears were enlarged until they could take the full-sized ear-plugs of grown men.

For girls there was little education in Inca times. They were intended only to be wives. Even the Sun Maidens were not taught about state organization, but only spinning, weaving, and embroidery. Because they specialized in such work, they became very skilled. The cloths which they wove were the best in the empire.

Such skills were not for the ordinary girls, who had to do their weaving in between pot-making, cooking, looking after their little brothers, and all the domestic chores of primitive society. They were not even allowed to have a say in the choice of their husbands. When they were of the right age, the town authorities told them whom they should marry, and what their allowance of material for household use would be.

They were given two years' exemption from paying taxes after the birth of each baby. The Incas realized that a busy housewife cannot do extra work while tiny children are crawling around her feet—and much more than all the taxes, the Incas wanted to have more Peruvian citizens growing up happily. That could only be done if every child in the empire was welcomed by its parents. The freedom from taxes for two years was a great help toward making people happier and more comfortable in their lives.

The Incas had a wonderful set of names for children at different ages: Infant-in-the-cradle, Learning-to-walk, Those-who-play, Big-Boys-and-Girls-who-begin-to-grow-up, and then, Young-People. At every age the taxes were altered, but as the family paid more of their produce to the Inca and the Sun, so their allowance of land was increased. It was all managed by the state. People had very little freedom, yet in studying the old reports of the conquistadores it seems that the people were happy enough. It is very likely that the laws were used for the benefit of the families in the villages. For example, if a son married, his land was kept with the family land, and his house was built in the same village.

The same kind of freedom was allowed in the matter of the tribute payments, since the people responsible for the reports and collection were local people.

In this way the Inca made sure that their rule was not a foreign oppression, but a natural part of the lives of the people.

Quipus were used as a means of checking on everything which people produced, but there were just as many quipus which recorded payments to people in distress and to the helpless and afflicted. Again, there was no special office to help the maimed and blind, but the local officials had to account for them and grant tax allowances according to rule. They also had to see that the special gifts from the stores of the Inca were properly distributed to those in need. Everything was recorded, but it all depended upon the local people whether the Inca system worked well or not.

Occasionally they might be visited by an Inca official who would have the quipus brought out and question the people about the facts behind the figures, but any sensible village headman was prepared for such a visitation, and in any case the inspectors were very careful and cautious in their approach. It was dangerous to accuse anyone if the case was to be tried before the judges. If the accusation proved wrong, the accuser paid the penalty which would have been paid by the accused if he had been guilty.

There was very little real poverty in Inca Peru, and those in need were well provided for, but there was also very little self-reliance. The people had done nothing to make the Inca laws. The whole of the system which helped them to live comfortably was given to them from above. The wisdom of Inca laws was the wisdom of a series of all-powerful kings who had the good sense to listen to the advice of their tutors whenever they were in doubt. Freedom? What was freedom in Inca Peru? Even the Inca was tied by inexorable law.

Within the law, and yet separate from the normal working of things, there was a class of people who lifted themselves out of the usual humdrum ways of life by special skills in healing and foretelling future events. These were more often than not wise women. They observed plants, animals, and people, and learned what made them act in unusual ways. The changes in the weather could be prophesied in this way, but the words did not look like a weather forecast; the wise woman would just tell the farmer which day would be the most lucky for him to do some special work.

With illness, too, there was a great deal of good scientific observation of the effects of herbs, but no medicine was given to a sick person merely as a scientific prescription; it was given with chants and drumming to drive out the spirits causing the sickness. This was good psychology, since the patient would recover much quicker if he was sure that his spirit was strengthened as well as his body. Then every improvement made by the medicine in the bodily comfort of the patient was felt as a strengthening of his mind also.

Sometimes lots were thrown with beans to foretell the future, and this could be controlled to some extent by the person who threw them. It was very different from the magic procedure of the priests who inspected the lungs of sacrificed animals, but to a superstitious people the presence of a medicine woman in a village could be a great comfort. It was more homely than the great ceremonies of the formal religion in the town.

It may be that the Inca regulations made life too dull for many people, and that would explain the hold which coca chewing had over them. They all carried little woolen bags filled with the dried leaves of the coca shrub. If they worked very hard, chewing coca helped them to keep up their energy. They forgot they were tired, and kept on. If they were hungry they felt comforted by the hazy stupor of the coca drug.

Unhappily, too many of them took to this habit, and we hear of rows of porters sitting down with inflamed eyes and stupid faces chewing themselves into insensibility until a shouted order brought them to their feet to carry their loads like a row of automata. Such drug-taking was not to relieve the pains of real want, for none need go hungry in Inca Peru, but to kill the misery of thinking.

Many a mitimae must have dreamed of the people in the old home, many a young couple must have longed for the partners whom they really wanted to marry. Many a parent sighed for the child taken from home to a higher education and social importance. Many an Inca must have wished to escape from the round of ceremonies.

But from the endless routines recorded in the knots

of the quipus there was only one relief, the peaceful days of old age in which one paid no taxes and enjoyed freedom from the regulations. Coca chewing provided only a temporary escape from monotony, and it often led to ill health and early death. What a pity that the Incas could not give people freedom to live!

The only control of coca addiction seems to have been the pressure of public opinion. The same applied to drunkenness. At the great festivals the Peruvians drank too much. They were quite aware that they would stagger around and start fights between clan and clan; but they could not give up the idea of drinking their beloved chicha, which was simply a fermented maize beer. It was related to the maize spirit and so was holy, to be drunk in particular at the planting festivals of the new crop. If a man committed a crime when drunk he was treated more leniently, because it was not so much he who did it as the divine spirit which had got inside him.

Apparently one of the wiser Incas tried to experiment by using smaller keros of liquor at the planting festival, but the whole population of Cuzco objected and sang insulting songs about him. Next year the offering-vases of the precious drink were larger than ever before.

In other matters Inca law was terribly simple and strict. There were no prisons. Thieves lost their hands. Cheats and perjurers might have their lips cut away. To conspire against an official might result in loss of the tongue and lopping off of the ears. Speaking ill of the Inca was a capital crime, and the offender was strangled. In cases of adultery, the man was bound and thrown over a cliff, while the woman was beaten to death.

There was no appeal from the sentence of a judge, but the trials seem to have been very fair. If a false judgment was discovered, the judge suffered the same punishment that he had inflicted, and also lost his office. When a criminal was punished by mutilation so that he could no longer earn his living, it was considered that his condition was natural. In that case he would be supported by his community, and the amount of food and clothing he needed was remitted from the tax paid to the Inca. The Incas preferred to keep such criminals alive, so that other people should see their sad condition and be warned. The judgments were recorded in numbers on quipus.

In Guaman Poma's book, the Quipu-camayoc stands by another counting device in which twenty squares are arranged in four columns; each vertical column contains either one, two, three, or five spots. In each square there are black and white spots. This seems to be a reckoning device with great possibilities, since one can change the rhythms of the black and white something like a thousand times. It might be possible by a mathematical analysis for us to work out the method of using this counting-board.

To the Peruvians it would have presented no difficulty. It was just the kind of thing which they habitually used in their weaving. When four colors are used in a weaving pattern they can be combined in the same pattern in twenty-four different arrangements. A Peruvian weaver would be unhappy unless all these possibilities had been explored. It seems that the mind of the nation turned toward mathematics, and that the quipu records were as natural to their way of thinking as alphabetic symbols are to us. Numbers were of tremendous interest to them and played a great part in their daily life, even in their religion.

A Quipu-camoyac working with a counting board.

the sacred huacas

HUACA IS a Quechua word which can be translated by "strange," "holy," "mysterious," and a dozen other somewhat similar words. It applied to lucky stones worn in a necklace as much as to the golden image of the Inca gods. An ancient pot was "huaca," and so was the rainbow.

In fact anything at all could be full of strange magic powers to the ancient Peruvians. They had lucky charms of all kinds, and watched the flight of birds to tell them what their fortune was going to be for the day.

The people did not think of a scientific universe in which everything was material. Their attitude was exactly the opposite; to them, everything had a kind of

121

spirit in it. There were great beings full of power, such as the glorious warm sun and the ever-changing moon. The winds came like flying serpents spreading blessings or disaster according to their natures. Spirits slipped into stones and made them take strange forms. Little fairy-like beings among the flowers whispered messages for those who could hear.

To the Incas, the whole of creation was a wonderland in which mankind tried to find a way. But always helping them was the rainbow. The rainbow of many colors was a promise of rain or sun for the crops; it showed all colors against the stormy blackness in the sky, and so it became a special symbol of the creator Viracocha.

Some of the great beings of the past, it was believed, had been turned into rocks. Huanacauri, the elder brother of the Incas who had come from the mountains with them, was turned into a column of stone and could still be seen only about six miles from Cuzco. He was always alive, and gave answers to questions through the mouths of the priests who attended him. Naturally he was the particular totem of his relatives, and most Incas asked his advice before they undertook any great new enterprise. But Huanacauri was quite capable of coming to visit his relatives, and often appeared to the Incas in dreams to warn them or to encourage them.

At first look all this seems a rather silly superstition, but psychologists will tell you that dreams reflect much of your own unconscious thoughts about life . . . the things which you often forget to think about while you are awake.

It seems that the Incas must have often seen the other side of themselves in visions while they slept, but instead of being frightened of the dark shadow, they felt it was somehow related to them and interpreted it to be their ancient kinsman Huanacauri, with a message for them. That Huanacauri usually gave very wise advice shows that the average Topa Inca was a thoughtful man, and that within his mind he was unconsciously working out problems and getting sound answers.

You may have had those lovely dreams in which you float through the air without effort, or swim in a great sea of water which has no resistance. The ancient Peruvians had exactly the same kind of dreams, but they went out of their way to explain them by supposing that some good fairy had taken them to see what was happening far off while they were asleep. If these dreams showed them things which came true later on, they told their dreams and were looked on as being specially blessed by the gods.

But there were also some very unpleasant little demons in Peruvian belief. They brought dreams which made people think they were breaking the laws. You have had dreams about finding yourself in some situation where you felt really shocked and shy, or those horrible dreams where one goes into a dark and frightening building, only to find himself on the edge of a precipice, or—still worse—peering at a doorway beyond which lurks some dark thing he is afraid to look at. You can well imagine what the simple Indians of Peru felt about such things. These dreams were the product of their own minds, but they did not know that, so they imagined that demons had taken their souls away to frighten them.

Guaman Poma de Ayala shows a good many of the little spirits which the Peruvians believed in, but he has usually given them horns and a tail, as the Spanish missionaries had suggested to him. They pop up from out of a magician's fire, or take offerings of drink from the Inca and fly on their bats' wings to give them to the sun. The native people really thought of them as devils.

One story tells of some young people who actually fell in love and told the town authorities that they should marry them, whether they were on the official lists of people to be married or not. This was completely shocking to the authorities. The young people were questioned and tortured. Eventually the boys confessed that spirits had flown down to them and given them little round transparent stones which would make the girls follow them wherever they wished. And sure enough, when the girls were questioned each one was found to have a transparent quartz pebble in her possession.

The Peruvians would permit love charms, but when

it came to charms which made people question the wisdom of the authorities it was altogether too much. The victims of this terrible magic were killed, and the demons were banished from Peru by very great magical ceremonies in which even the Inca burned all the small huacas which he had in his personal collection.

However, the huacas were never absent for long. In many ways they were the important gods to the ordinary people. The good luck and bad luck of every day interested the village farmers of Peru. The great magic of the changing seasons was well enough known to them, but they would never think of working out for themselves when they should plant or reap. The priests of the Sun set the times for these festivals, and after the Inca had taken the first step, every farmer in the country felt that he should do the same. They were not even very interested in the stars and planets, but preferred only to notice the moon when it was full and luminous. They were afraid of the dark and did not often go about at night. Even after a festival, if they were out late, they would wrap up in a warm piece of cloth and sleep in any doorway in the town rather than travel back to the village in the darkness.

The official religion was much more complex, but when we remember that the rock pillar of Huanacauri was a relative of the Incas we have to be prepared for very strange sights. Near Cuzco was a rock, the Kenko stone, which looked roughly like a great puma. A puma was a dangerous animal when angered, so this great

A puma.

rock became linked in people's minds with the savage
and brave nature of the puma itself. This in turn linked
it with the warriors. The Inca had a wall built around
the base of the stone and a space cleared in front of
it, so that people could make offerings to the lucky
rock on great occasions. The Inca himself poured out
the offering and led the chants to the puma spirits.

There were many legends in Peru about people who
had been turned into stone, or of gigantic animals
which had been similarly transformed by their first
ancestors. Their petrified remains were often pointed
out among the rocks. A very interesting discovery was
made not long ago in a remote valley some seventy
miles inland from Lima. At this site—named Masma by

Dr. Daniel Ruzo who discovered it—there is a complex wall of hard gray limestone under which a mass of volcanic rock was at one time thrust. The lava had burst forth in rolling, contorted forms, and then cooled. Rains and frosts of the mountains had also done their work, with the result that the Masma Valley is surrounded by formations of fantastic rocks.

There are cliffs sculptured into great heads and faces, rocks like giant lizards, sudden outcrops of limestone that look like isolated castles with human figures on their battlements. The Indians were unable to leave these natural wonders alone. At some early period they tried to increase the resemblances by touching them up here and there with a little sculptural work.

A pottery vessel representing a puma with jaws open.

In the end the sacred place became so full of this mixture of natural forms and sculpture that at certain times of the day and on definite dates of the year the sun's rays fell at the right angles to emphasize the shape of one or other of the supposed figures of the ancient huacas. It was probably a place where the priests determined the calendar for the year by noting the days on which certain rocks received the first rays of the sun. Even now, when the people of the towns in the valley celebrate the festival of the patron saint of their church, they like to go halfway up the slope leading to this valley of the giants and hold the meeting which organizes the processions and ceremonies. They start the new year by coming down from the mountain to the town, just as was done in ancient times.

What gods were worshiped in this valley? This was an important place, because the mountains at its rim form the watershed between the streams which flow westward into the Pacific at Lima and those flowing eastward to join the Amazon. We have a document written in 1608 by Father Francisco de Avila, in which he describes the ancient religion of the people who lived here and repeats a curious legend about Viracocha in his form of Koniraya.

Koniraya was a creator god who suffered many misadventures from which he extricated himself by magic. He represented the trickster figure found in many primitive religions. The Indians of Huarochiri remember him in connection with his treatment of the animals which helped or hindered him. If one compares the legend with the figures in the rock it becomes possible to see the story pictured there. Of course one has to use a lot of imagination, but so did the ancient people.

To date there are no reports of pottery found near the "touched up" rocks in the Masma Valley. Possibly it was always as shown in the pictures by Poma de Ayala, where offerings were poured out from wooden keros, and not from pottery vessels.

Just as the sun illuminated different rocks in the mountain valleys at different times of the year, so it was used by skilled astronomer-priests to mark the seasons in the Inca cities. There is hardly a town without its sun throne, Intihuatana, in all the Inca Empire.

An Inca astronomer-priest studying the patterns of light on a sun throne.

These thrones are really sundials used for measuring the days of the year rather than the hours of the day.

The special sun festival of the Inca family was the June solstice when the sun was farthest away to the north. There were moments of anxiety; perhaps the god might continue his journey and not return as he usually did. However, as the sun rose on the next morning he would shine into the doorway of the Coricancha as usual. The Topa Inca and the High Priest would be there by the altar. The High Priest would hold a concave metal mirror to focus the sun's rays on a bunch of fiber. The concentrated heat would set it alight, and the Inca would give the new fire to his people.

One can check the calendar very exactly by noting which stars are on the horizon at sunset and sunrise each day. In the clear mountain air of Cuzco this was comparatively easy; so a star calendar was used, and stars held their proper place in the golden wall of the Coricancha. Between the stars moved mysterious birds which we should call the planets. Their movements were very carefully checked, especially the wonderfully brilliant little sun, the planet Venus, which was counted as two beings, the Morning Star and the Evening Star.

We have no record of what powers were ascribed to the stars and planets in ancient Peruvian astrology, but we may be sure that the people of the Inca Empire were not at all behind other races in believing that they could read their fates in the stars.

130

However, the religion of the Incas was by no means just an astronomical fable. There was a definite set of stories behind their beliefs, and these had some moral purpose within them—a kind of poem about the creation of the world and the appearance of the first human beings. It was a system of belief in the Creator and his dealings with men.

If the beliefs about the origins of the mountains and rivers and the reason why the animals had their various markings were often absurd, they were no more so than other primitive superstitions. Mankind demands that the gods should be responsible for every detail of creation. The Sun was father of the Incas, and Lord of Gold, but he was entirely subservient to the greater power of the creator Viracocha.

The stately dance of the sun, moon, and planets in the sky never appeared mechanical to the Peruvians. They saw it as the movement of living beings who were concerned with the affairs of earth. In all things they felt that man and the world of Nature were interlinked. This feeling is certainly much older than Inca times in Peru. On the coast near Nasca there are some rocky hills where men made great figures of flying birds, associated with straight lines which appear to have reference to some astronomical bearing. We have no doubt that the birds represented the planets; so at least six centuries before the Incas there were astronomers in Peru who were so enthusiastic that they laid out their work in boulders carefully placed on the hilltops in a pattern so big that it is not visible on the ground. This was only discovered from aerial photographs.

How such a thing could have been planned, since the people making it could never have seen the whole design, is quite a problem. A guess would make the original pattern a piece of tapestry, because the shape of the birds is exactly the shape of birds in Nasca tapestries. If one took a measurement of one pace of about twenty inches for every thread in the tapestry shape, the result would be that a bird four inches wide on the tapestry would be expanded to about one hundred and twenty feet.

Yet it would need a very skilled man to lay out such a design without being able to see how well he was working. He had no aeroplane, as we have, to see the perfection of the designs he made. Since the figures contain no recognizable bearings within themselves, it is likely that they were placed among the stone alignments of the observatory simply as an offering to the planets. Perhaps the planners wished to show them their own images to make them pleased with mankind.

However, the astronomers and the great lords of the Incas were all at one in the end; they faced the road to death with hope of a future. From ancient vases one sees that there was a land of the dead in which the skeletons of the departed Peruvians danced and sang for joy. There was a great willingness among these people to accept their fate. If things went wrong in life there was no resentment. One was simply moving with the stream of fate. When death came, it was for the survivors to weep for the loss of one whom they had known so long. For the dying person there was the warm hope of descending the dark pathway, and then, after breaking away from this world, an entrance to the land where one could meet all the friends and relatives who had gone there before.

There was a strong belief that the dead re-appeared on earth; sometimes in dreams to warn or advise their relatives, but sometimes, too, as apparitions. Ghosts were not very popular. People feared them and felt there was something wrong with a person who wanted to come back to this earth, where the passing of time made it but a place of sorrow.

Nevertheless, they expected that one day they would all be reborn to come to live on earth again. Of course, this was for people who had lived well and done their duty to their neighbors. For the evil-livers there was no particular hell, but utter destruction. For them no sun, no flowers, no drinking and dancing—just nothing, nothing at all. So one hoped not to be among those who were lost.

We do not know how these people fared, but we do know that their history records many brave and noble lives. As for their discarded bodies, few have survived in good condition, and many of these have been taken away to repose on the shelves of museums. It is always moving to see the quiet bodies wrapped in their fine clothes, awaiting a new life; so patiently they seem to sleep there, just waiting.

the end and
the beginning

LATE IN APRIL, 1532, the Spaniards under Pizarro landed at the port of Tumbez. There were one or two minor skirmishes, that was all. After two weeks, Pizarro gathered his little army together and went on an exploring journey. At the beginning of June he decided to settle at San Miguel de Piura, as he named it, a pleasant valley town beside a river which opened into the Pacific. If needed, ships could come from Tumbez to assist him or evacuate the army.

But nothing whatever happened; the local people were friendly and happy, and flocked to meet the strangers and exchange presents; although they did not understand, they listened to the proclamation that their country was now part of the dominions of the Emperor of Spain.

On September 24th, Pizarro decided to leave San Miguel. He had sent a good supply of gold home to Spain, but his men were spoiling for some kind of action. Fifty of them stayed to garrison San Miguel, and the rest, less than two hundred, set out to conquer the empire of the Incas.

At Caja they sent Hernando de Soto to visit an Inca chieftain who lived nearby. Again for ten days nothing happened; then De Soto came back with the Inca general and a load of presents carried on the backs of servants. With it came a message from Atahuallpa Inca that he would welcome the Spanish visitors if they came across the mountains to see him where he was encamped at the warm springs beside the town of Caxamalca. Pizarro accepted the invitation, and sent back presents for Atahuallpa.

Already the Spaniards had heard a good deal about the war in which the prince of Quito had conquered the lord of Cuzco. It seems that they had no conception of the rights and wrongs of the case, and did not attempt to represent themselves as the friends of Topa Inca Huascar. Hundreds of members of the Inca family, perhaps thousands, had been killed by Atahuallpa. He had determined that there should be no opposition to his rule from any of his jealous relatives. He kept Huascar in prison apparently for the purpose of making him feel his unhappy position all the more keenly. But the Spaniards knew only that they were faced by a great leader of armies who had overthrown a rival for the throne and was now enjoying his victory with his soldiers around him. They had good reason to feel nervous about the outcome of their visit to such a mighty king.

The people of the coasts had supported Huascar in the war, but had accepted defeat. It may well be that they did not resist Pizarro because they felt that he would avenge the captivity of the Topa Inca. But why Atahuallpa made no move for five months, even when the Spaniards took over control of towns and seized the supplies of sacred gold, we do not know. Perhaps he knew he could crush such a small body of bearded white men whenever he wished, and was waiting to celebrate the purification festival in the October moon, when he would cleanse the land of invaders in the same way as of any other pestilence.

Or perhaps he recognized the magical meaning of a new visitation of white men with beards as a message from Viracocha, and relied on his influence with the god, who after all was a relative, to have them adopted into his service, thus making him still greater. We shall probably never know exactly why Atahuallpa calmly waited for his visitors to come to him.

The Spaniards advanced rather cautiously. When they came to the difficult passes through the mountains they expected to be ambushed at any moment. They knew they were in a position where nothing could save them if they were attacked from the higher ground. But no; nothing happened, and as they rode

137

on to the plateau they found they were approaching a wonderful paved road, far finer than anything they had seen in Spain.

In the distance were more mountains with snowy peaks. A river led through the plain, and far away they could distinguish a cloud over the hot springs. Through increasing numbers of villages they approached the city. Then they saw the camp of the Incas. Tents and bivouacs covered a vastly greater area than the city itself. Half a million warriors were there. The Spaniards knew in their hearts that they were walking into a trap, but Pizarro calmly accepted the situation and pressed on.

On the evening of November 15th, Pizarro entered the city of Caxamalca. The Inca received him in near silence, explaining that this was a fast day before the festival on the morrow. He assigned buildings in the town to be occupied by the Spaniards. At last Pizarro felt that he had stone walls around him, and when he left the Inca that night his plans were ready. The stone houses would form a base for his men. As the Inca entered the great square the horsemen would advance on both sides to welcome him. Then the arquebusiers would cover the retreat as the Inca was seized and made captive.

The plan was wild enough, but it was literally the only chance the Spaniards had to remain alive and extricate themselves from the trap. It was as if a fly

Pizarro leading his men through the Peruvian mountains.

should plan to escape from the spider's web by eating the spider.

On the morning of November 15th, 1532, the Inca Atahuallpa was seized in the midst of the greatest nobles of his empire and a great part of his army. The appearance of horsemen, something never seen before by the Incas, and the thunderous crash of the clumsy arquebuses demoralized all opposition. Although the Inca soldiers made a brave rally, the square gave them no room to maneuver, and they were cut to pieces by repeated charges of the armored Spaniards, who were immune to the blows of the bronze-headed maces of the Peruvians. The slaughter was terrible, and in the end the Inca remained the prisoner of his reckless opponents.

The captivity of Atahuallpa Inca was not made hard. He was kept within the palace at Caxamalca, but allowed visits from his officials and the company of his favorite wives. During this period Pizarro visited the great temple of Pachacamac and destroyed the old wooden idol. In its place he set up a cross on top of the great brick pyramid. The priests had hidden away a good deal of the gold from the temple, but Pizarro took a rich booty all the same. Then he found out about Topa Inca Huascar. He returned to Atahuallpa and demanded an explanation of events, thinking that he should be able to control the country by playing off one faction against the other. But next day he heard that Huascar had been killed by drowning.

Atahuallpa had sized up the Spaniard very well, and explained that it was not by his orders that Huascar had been killed but by the mistaken hurry of his soldiers. Meanwhile he offered to pay a ransom for himself in gold, which should fill the chamber he was in as high as a mark nine feet up on the wall. Pizarro accepted.

Three soldiers were sent to golden Cuzco to command the stripping of gold from the palaces and the Coricancha, for the ransom of Atahuallpa Inca. From the Coricancha came nine hundred plates of gold as big as the lid of a wooden chest. The mummies of the dead Incas were left. As the commissioners returned with their loads, news came of the landing of more Spaniards. Atahuallpa felt that his fate was sealed, for now there were more enemies come to demand gold. He saw a bright comet in the sky, and told his attendants that he must die soon. The Spaniards said that from that hour he became quiet and serious, as if preparing for his end.

It soon happened as he expected. The Spaniards wanted to divide the treasure before all of it was delivered. Then, amid their own quarrels, they heard of the massing of Inca armies around them. The treasure in their hands was worth about 33,600,000 dollars in present values.

Atahuallpa quietly demanded his freedom. The Spaniards decided they must hold him longer. Rumors of the Indian rising grew, and Atahuallpa was put in

141

chains. A trumped-up charge was made against him, even though some brave men dared to say that the Inca who had treated them so well should not be murdered. However, he was sentenced to be burned alive. Atahuallpa broke down at this, but the Spaniards told him that if he would consent to be baptized they would only strangle him with the garrote. Atahuallpa accepted this grotesque mercy, and died peacefully. The date was August 29th, 1533.

The next Spanish move was a five-hundred-mile march to Cuzco. The Inca Empire was falling into ruins all around them. The outlying provinces revolted and started to fight one another. The home organization broke down. Some sections of the army remained in existence and harassed the Spaniards, but the great general Chalcuchima was caught and burned alive; he died laughing at them and calling on Pachacamac. From later history it would seem that his wish for revenge was gratified.

On November 15th, 1533, Pizarro entered Cuzco. The army noticed the wonderful building of the great Sacsahuaman fortress and the round tower for water storage in the center, the foundations of which have only recently been discovered. They saw the rows of palaces facing the narrow street and noted that the doorways were brilliantly painted. But there was still gold in Cuzco; and in spite of the order to preserve the ancient city, the troops burst into the palaces and temples to loot everything they could find.

Wooden cup, inlaid with mastic picture of Inca nobles wearing elaborate feather headdresses.

Later they robbed the ordinary houses, and sought out the graveyards, where they turned the mummies out of their vaults and stripped them of their rich ornaments. Caves in the hills were searched for treasure, and then the whole mass was piled in the great square of the city and divided up. Another eight or nine million dollars' worth of gold was taken away, and Golden Cuzco was left desolate to become a provincial Spanish town.

The fantastic destruction of the Inca Empire continued all along the line. The Spaniards found that all organization had broken down, and they were faced with the problem of re-creating some sort of order within the country. But it was only with the help of local governors and Quipu-camayocs that they were able to rebuild enough of the central government to carry on.

The Spanish version of the feudal system fitted the situation quite well. Leading Spaniards were given towns with the land belonging to them. They appointed the officials of a town council, and saw to it that the Indians living on the land brought in material as it was needed. They did not know that in most cases it was less than the Incas had demanded. They continued the old system by which every town was responsible for the roads and bridges leading to it, and then they started to decide who was entitled to the greatest honors in this new country which they had seized. One after another they plotted and rioted in attempts to seize power. The fiercest contestants were Almagro and Pizarro, the two men who had done most to win the country for Spain.

In the midst of this, Manco, the young heir to the Inca throne, was stung to revolt. Silently he organized a resistance movement, and then when the time was ripe he assaulted the city. The place was set on fire. For four days the blaze continued, Peruvian warriors wrecking in despair the palaces of their ancestors. Only the great buildings near the center of the city survived. The Spanish garrison fought back bravely and withstood a siege of five months, every day with some outbreak of bitter fighting. But in the end harvest time came, and the Spaniards awoke to see that the enemy army had almost disappeared overnight. The farmers had gone home to reap their crops to feed their families. The Empire of the Incas was finished so far as they were concerned.

Inca Manco ruled a while from the mountains, but he was hunted down. Meanwhile the conquerors became more and more involved in their personal hatreds, and at last the whole unhappy business broke out into a series of civil wars. Eventually the Spanish government intervened, and sent the Viceroy Mendoza from Mexico. Though he only lived a few months, he brought peace and order to the country, and arranged for the honorable burial of the remains of Pizarro and Almagro and the other conquistadores who had been killed in the civil wars.

After the strife ended, the development of Peru was hindered by terrible epidemics of plague and fevers, but gradually the country came to its feet again. By 1600 it was already rich and prosperous, with many newly built towns. All the original conquerors were gone to their graves, and people remembered them as turbulent heroes of another, more brutal age.

The Incas remained. No Topa Inca was left, but seven hundred Inca nobles lived in Peru with the rank of Spanish noblemen. They came to the Viceroy's court in their own national costume wearing beautiful Inca embroideries. For another century this tradition remained, and there are some portraits of a few of these nobles as late as the early eighteenth century, still wearing the traditional dress of the Children of the Sun.

Slowly the remains of Inca Peru grew into Spanish Peru. Cuzco was partly rebuilt, but was never again the capital. The old temples were gone, but the Inca roads were used, and Indian peasants tilled the fields or became servants on the great Spanish estates. Along the coast the Chimu potters went on making pottery in the ancient way. But instead of depicting the Morning Star being seized by the Sun Puma, they modeled Christian marytrs being seized by curly-maned Roman lions. Their knowledge increased so that they began to use green glaze over the ancient pots. But the change was so gradual that there are many archaeological problems left to be solved if we are to understand the very slow

Wooden kero beaker. Design represents the sacred puma with
a condor-head tail.

changes in the way of life of the Peruvian Indians.

Later, in the eighteenth century, Spain fell upon bad times and the colonies were bled of all their resources to pay for the wars in which the country was involved. At last, when the Napoleonic wars in Europe gave the opportunity, the first stirrings of revolt broke out and then Peru followed the flag of the liberator Bolívar and declared her independence.

The road to freedom was a hard one, and the busy commercial life of the nineteenth century separated the Indians of the highlands still further from the townsfolk of the cities. But as prosperity returned, so the unity of the new Peruvian people was steadily built up.

A new respect for the wonderful past of the Indians, as well as for their modern music and folklore, has begun to bring them once more into the world of high culture. Many a Peruvian poet is now writing verse in the old Runa Simi, or Quechua language. In a sense which they never imagined, the Incas are returning to their ancient land. The archaeological record is enlightening the modern life of the people.

We are all, to some extent, heirs to Inca Peru. The Incas left us invaluable gifts in the potato, for food, quinine, for medicine, and alpaca, for clothing. Their sense of color and design influences many modern artists, and their ancient songs have been echoed knowingly by modern composers.

One must remember that nice little animal whom

the Incas called Cui Cui. If you want to know what the little Cui Cui has done for humanity, ask any doctor how the guinea pig has helped modern medical research. The nutria, whose name is so well known in the fur trade, is another Peruvian animal. Among the flowers we have the colorful petunia and the fuchsia from the Peruvian mountains.

There is not very much gold now from Peru, but silver, tin, lead, and zinc come from the mines, and copper is produced in great quantities. Near Nasca, seams of coal have been developed, while the water power of the rushing mountain streams has now begun to provide electric power for a Peru which promises to become a land richer than the Incas ever dreamed it would be.

epilogue

WE HAVE LOOKED at an ancient civilization and found out some things about it which we did not know before; but we have not kept strictly to archaeology—we have called in other sciences to our aid all along the line. When we looked at the Inca gods we found that the psychologists could help our inquiries. When we considered the balsa rafts, we found that navigators had interesting advice to give us. We were puzzled for dates and found that the physicists could tell us about carbon 14.

To be a successful archaeologist nowadays, it is not sufficient to provide simply a detailed plan and sections of an archaeological site, together with everything that was found in it. This is all very interesting and may lead to valuable discovery, but how much

151

more important it becomes if we gather together a team of experts to examine our material and report upon it. New ways of looking at the same thing bring out new aspects of value.

In the Peruvian field we are not lacking in examples of this kind of thing. For one example we can look at the teeth of the Peruvian mummies in a museum. Some of them have inlays of gold and turquoise. What a difficult ordeal it must have been to have one's teeth scraped down to take an inlay! Probably they deadened the pain with coca leaves, and worked while the great warrior, who wanted such a fine decoration, slept under the drug. Some of these teeth were submitted to dentists in Sweden, who examined the dental cement used. It is still as firm today as it was when new. The basic cement contained mercuric oxide. This is poisonous unless strictly controlled in small amounts in safe places, but it is used also in modern dental cements. It has also been proved that the ancient Peruvian dentists had conducted careful research with such good effect that they were able to use other poisonous substances for the good of their patients.

Another piece of research on the microscopic structure of metals was conducted on an ancient Peruvian copper ball. The joint was proved to have been welded. Working with a blowpipe on the metal heated in a charcoal fire, as we know the Peruvians did, it is almost impossible to weld copper. The metal oxidizes and burns away before it melts. The answer appears to have been that the joint of the ball was buried in close-packed powdered charcoal, which absorbs the oxygen, and so the craftsman was able to heat up a tiny portion at a time for welding in safety. That single specimen is a proof of the almost incredible technical skill of Peruvian metal smiths.

Weaving was one of the special skills of the ancient Peruvians. Using a simple back-strap loom, the weavers could reproduce all the techniques for which we construct elaborate mechanical looms. An examination of some of the fabrics to find out what dyes were used proved that the people of the hot coastlands grew natural cotton in two colors: one white, and the other pale green. It may be that the colored cotton plant was at first a "freak," but at least someone in the past noted that green cotton plant, and carefully bred from it so that there were sufficient plants for the weaving industry of the coastal towns.

On the other hand, researchers sometimes take most unusual lines to find out unexpected things for the sake of purely modern knowledge. Several Peruvian mummies are now being examined to determine their blood groupings. Little sections of desiccated muscle are being taken and gently teased apart in distilled water. In some of the bigger muscles there are dried-up blood vessels with some of the blood cells still intact. These can be examined microscopically and subjected to reaction tests which yield a reliable estimate of the blood group of the individuals examined.

So archaeology is continually opening up new wonders, because it can be brought into line with all the other sciences. It always holds an interest for the future—even for the politician, who can prove or disprove theories from the study of what happened under the Inca system of complete control of the daily life of the whole population. It can also warn mankind by showing the destruction caused by past wars, or by neglect of the food crops, or still more important, by neglect of the drains and the consequent ravages of epidemics.

The archaeologist can show how the climate of our earth has been changing in the last few thousand years, and how mankind has adapted to the changing circumstances. It illuminates the words of the historians, proving them or disproving them with complete impartiality. Yet it remains the most human of the sciences, because it reflects the way people have lived, what they have made for themselves, and what they have believed, over the thousands of years of human development.

Eventually our own times will become the subject of archaeology. It is surprising how rapidly the years slip into the forgotten past. As we are aware that our own world is changing, we can reflect that there will be much of interest in what we leave behind for the men of the future to discover. I wonder how they will think of us in comparison with the Incas of Peru.

PHOTOGRAPH CREDITS:

index

addiction, by Incas to the coca drug, 117-118

Almagro, 101, 145

Amazon jungle, 16, 35; R., 39, 128

Ancon, pre-Inca cemetery at, 24

andenes, farming methods on, 62-65, 69

Andes Mountains, 11, 15, 30

Antisuyu (eastern region of Inca Peru), 70

Araucanian Indians, the, 38

archaeological discoveries, importance of, 154; of Inca buildings, 20-21; of the Inca coastal highway, 78; of Inca pottery in the Galapagos Islands, 99; interrelationship with other sciences, 151-154; of Julio C. Tello, 25-26; at Macchu Pichu, 68-70; of pottery, 18-20; of rock formations in the Masma Valley, 126-129

astronomy, Inca knowledge of, 107-108; relation to Inca religious practices, 129-130

Atahuallpa, 87-88, 136-138, 140-142

Atlantic Ocean, 39

Austria, 106

Avila, Father Francisco de, 128

Ayala, Don Felipe de, 9-10

Ayala, Guaman Poma de, ms. of, 9-23, 32, 88, 105-106, 119, 124, 129

Bandelier, 40

Bingham, Prof. Hiram, 68

boat-building, of balsa rafts by the Chimu people, 96-99; in a pre-historic Peruvian coastal village, 31; of totora reed canoes by the Chimu people, 95

Bolívar, 148

bridge building, in the Inca highlands, 74-77

British Guiana, 102

burial of the dead, in the Colla culture, 41; in the Nasca culture, 27; in the Paracas culture, 34; of Topa Incas in special palaces, 50

Caja, 136

Calancha, Father, 110

Caribbean Sea, 102

Cauca R., Colombia, 102

Caxamalca, 136, 138, 140

Chalcuchima, 87-88, 142

Chan Chan, 92

Chanca confederacy of tribes (pre-Inca), 42

Chasquis (Inca runners), 80-81, 95

Chavín culture, in Peruvian highlands (pre-Inca), 34-35, 37

Chibcha Empire, Colombia, 102-103

Chile, 29, 101

Chimu people, on Peruvian coast, in Inca period, 89-101; in pre-Inca times, 39-40; under Spanish rule, 146

chumpi (vicuna cloth), 13

cities and towns, of the Chimu people, 39, 92-93; in the Inca highlands, 62-67

climate, of Inca Peru, 89, 101; of pre-historic Peru, 30

Colla people, in Peruvian highlands (pre-Inca), 41-42

Colombia, 102

157

158